Millionaire Mortgage Broker
Insider Tips, Tactics, and Ten-X Success

Get to Profit, Faster and Easier,
Arranging Commercial Real Estate Financing

Adam Petriella

SILVERTHREAD CAPITAL

First Printing, 2020

ISBN: 978-1-7352255-0-0

Silverthread Capital Corporation
555 Madison Avenue
Fifth Floor
New York, NY 10022
212-500-2087
www.SilverthreadCapital.com

CONTENTS

INTRODUCTION

IF I CAN DO IT, SO CAN YOU

Thank you for your interest in the practical aspects of arranging commercial real estate loans.

So why should you listen to me? If you are interested in how deal making works in commercial real estate, from the bottom up, then my hard-won advice can be beneficial to you. Here is a brief background profile of my values and experience.

My family had owned and operated a restaurant and tavern in the South Bronx since the 1920s. One of my favorite things in life was visiting my dad and his brother and the cast of characters there. In 1978, a fire ripped through the kitchen and the apartments upstairs. Among all the details I recall, what stand out the most are the inability of my father to gain any financial traction to get the business back up and running, and his inability to get a loan to buy the building then offered for sale. None of his friends or the bankers he knew would take a chance on a cash business in the South Bronx in the 1970s.

Because I value the hard work and dedication of independent businesspeople, one of my goals for entering the real estate business was to help small, entrepreneurial owners make better-informed real estate decisions. It was personal.

I've been in the investment real estate sales business and commercial real estate loan origination for over 25 years. My career began in Los Angeles with a small eight-office commercial real estate investment sales company that is now an international, publicly traded organization with close to 100 offices. I'm proud, in some small way, to have contributed to that growth.

After graduating from Cornell's Hotel School and putting in five years of working in the hotel business, I decided to move to Los Angeles to learn more about the commercial real estate sales business. Coming straight from the hospitality industry where most people are, well, hospitable, into the wild west of commercial real estate sales was equal parts exciting, frustrating, morally revealing (the subject of a future book), and lucrative.

Prior to moving to Los Angeles, I flipped a property netting $32,000 in 11 months, with an investment of only $500. But I knew nothing about real estate.

Following a 10-day training, I started cold calling, canvassing, doing valuations, and submitting proposals, and eventually I won listings and sold properties. Starvation was followed by several years of success until the market crashed in the early 1990s. Many of my friends were scared. They had mortgages and car payments, and none of us wanted to go broke again.

In years prior, when the president of the company invited me to consider joining the management team to learn how to run an office, I had declined. But with the market crashing and my financial obligations as they were, I agreed to enter the executive training track. Learning how to run a high-octane commercial real estate sales operation stretched me; what I thought was purely intuitive turned out to be much more calculated.

The responsibilities of the position included recruiting, training, and leading agents; ensuring compliance with company policy and real estate law and norms; staff hiring and direction; business planning; marketing and advertising; full P&L responsibility; dispute resolution; business development; event planning and presentations; competitor analysis; forecasting; and, most importantly, navigating through complex and thorny issues with intensely competitive, high earning, non-salaried, all-commission real estate agents. And that last responsibility was performed against the backdrop of stern advice from my boss: "Never lose a high-producing agent."

I went on to build some of the most successful offices in the company in Encino and Newport Beach, and I opened their first office in the New York Metro area. Some of the agents I hired and mentored went on to become top-earning agents. In one of my offices, we had 6 of the top 20 earning agents among a total of 1,500 agents companywide.

After 9/11, living in NYC was no longer an option. My wife, newborn, and I moved back to LA and I began all over, learning how to arrange financing for commercial real estate. *To my surprise, this was different in almost every way in comparison to my previous experience listing and selling properties.* I began a new adventure—again—knowing no one and nothing about what the heck I was doing! But what I did know was how to pick up the phone and use my knowledge about real estate to have a soft conversation to qualify any interest in financing.

My first database consisted of developers because they are *always* searching for capital. Within 30 days of starting I had a great conversation with a developer who had just finished a 103,000 square foot high tech office industrial, R&D campus looking to place permanent financing on the asset. With the help of a very generous friends, Anita and Jerry, I learned by doing and through osmosis. It took six months to close a very complicated transaction. The loan size was $19.8 million, and our fee was 83 basis points, a $164,340 fee! I was on my way to a million!

Before the 2008 crash, I closed many more deals, preferring the more complicated bridge and construction loans, staying away from multifamily because loans and Lenders and mortgage brokers were viewed as a commodity and fees were constantly compressed. Not fun. *But*, after the crash, Fannie Mae was about the only Lender that was open for business. I grudgingly began working small multifamily financing opportunities but eventually gained a tremendous amount of knowledge about the underwriting and credit decision-making process of a Lender whose exit was the sale of bonds; this was all so different from a credit union or conventional bank.

My volume was so good that in 2012 I left to form my own company with a partner I had hired right out of Loyola and who had been working as my associate for a year by then. He was and still is one of the best Intermediaries around!

In 2014, a recruiter called and invited me to meet with a start-up looking to develop a CRE loan origination platform. The start-up was funded by an alternative asset management fund, Waterfall Asset Management (WAM). WAM purchased seven Coldwell Banker Commercial franchises to serve as a lead source for loans into their lending platform, Ready Cap Commercial (RCC). I hired and managed a team of Intermediaries and participated in the origination and underwriting of loans slated for securitization or placement with RCC and other lending partners including credit unions, banks, commercial mortgage-backed securities (CMBS), insurance companies, and non-bank Lenders.

As you can see, my experience is unique, I love an interesting startup, and I get a lot of enjoyment from developing talent.

I've made mistakes and learned my lessons, and I'm willing to share these with you.

Hopefully, at least one concept or one thought will save you some time and frustration. It's my goal to provide you with ideas and *reality checks* that will help you shorten the learning curve.

Please note: This isn't a book about analyzing loans, although there is a section devoted to how we analyze a loan opportunity. It isn't a sales book either, but there is undoubtedly a component that is sales oriented.

Because time is our most valuable asset, I promise to provide you with actionable insights I've developed throughout my career. The most important concept I teach is assessing probability to avoid time-wasting traps. Learning probability can help you develop a client with a lifetime value worth millions to you.

My library consists of dozens of how-to, self-help, and motivational books. The ones I enjoy the most get to the point. Maybe it's a sign of my age. When I was younger and grasping for insights, I enjoyed the rambling stories familiar in so many how-to books. Honestly, I just don't have the time now, and I'm sure you don't either!

I hope to provide rich insights to help you succeed on your journey in this industry.

Silverthread Capital Corporation
www.Silverthreadcapital.com

My company, Silverthread Capital Corporation, arranges debt and equity for owners of commercial real estate in the $1MM to $100MM bracket.

Unlike companies with physical offices and staff, Silverthread is a remote platform. Yes, even pre-COVID we began building a remote business model. Silverthread Capital provides opportunities for motivated individuals seeking to exercise their skills, provide for themselves and their families, and have more freedom than most brokerage opportunities can provide. With the growing cultural acceptance of "work from anywhere" and the use of technology that we carry in our pockets and our half-inch thin laptops, intelligent Silverthread Capital Intermediaries assist their clients with *their knowledge, not their location.*

After you read this book or take my online course, (see www.SilverthreadcapitalU.com) if you'd like to discuss some opportunities with us, please feel free to email me at the following address: careers@silverthreadcapital.com.

Thank you for your time, and I hope you enjoy and profit from this book!

YOUR ROLE AS AN INTERMEDIARY

(COMMERCIAL REAL ESTATE MORTGAGE BROKER)

Let's begin by discussing a little bit about the role of an Intermediary. But first, let's clarify the term *mortgage broker* and how it's used. Some people in commercial real estate call themselves mortgage brokers, but it's easy to confuse us with a mortgage broker specializing in single-family residences—a very different business. Some people call themselves a broker, but this may confuse a client into thinking you are a leasing broker or a sales broker or a house sales broker. So, I suggest using the word *Intermediary* or the longer *commercial real estate mortgage broker.*

Intermediaries work for the Borrower, *not the Lender.* **Who are Borrowers?**

A Borrower is an individual or entity that owns or wants to own commercial and multifamily properties.

Hint: the best client who is seeking to buy a property has a deadline. The most common deadline is a 1031 tax deferred exchange.

First time buyers without a deadline are tire-kickers. Tire kickers will use Intermediaries to assess what amount of loan is available for properties they are seeking to buy, so they can calculate the amount of equity they need to contribute. And that's fine. This can be an excellent way to build a relationship.

However, beware: If a person has not purchased a property before, and there's no deadline such as a 1031 exchange, and they're kicking tires, that could be a great learning experience **if you have the time.**

If you're going to make millions as an Intermediary, one of the critical components is prospecting probable Borrowers. Please note, with few exceptions, Intermediaries are not paid a salary. *You must get going as quickly as possible to develop momentum and confidence.*

The role of an Intermediary is to develop an understanding of Borrower motivation; to know the characteristics of the four major asset classes and knowledge of the Lenders who provide investment real estate financing; and to make a match and guide the Borrower through the process.

In a perfect world, you would know every owner in your chosen geographic area—every shopping center owner, multifamily owner, office building owner, industrial building owner, and, perhaps in particular situations, hotel and motel owners in your area. If you're just starting in the business, though, I'd advise you to stick to smaller properties, such as a million-dollar loan.

The most activity nationwide in transactions, both on the sales and the financing, although they're not glamorous, are the $1 million to $10 million deals.

You'll see in the *Wall Street Journal* or your local business publications that people talk about the larger deals. If you're just starting, ignore those and go after the smaller properties. The probability of closing smaller properties is much higher in the most active part of the market.

Keep in mind that, unlike the infrequent sale of a property, financing a property can happen as frequently as every

three to five to seven years. Commercial real estate mortgages, unlike single-family residential mortgages, are not written as a 30-year fixed-term loan. I'll talk a little bit later about amortization, but most multifamily properties, for example, are amortized on a 30-year basis. However, the loan can be due and payable in 10 years (not 30), or the loan can be refinanced without penalty in five years.

The unique character of commercial loans provides us ample opportunity to make beneficial relationships with owners hoping to do repeat business throughout the relationship.

There are ample opportunities in the marketplace and versus sales, where for example, as a sales agent, I would have a thousand people in my database and maybe sell 10 properties a year. Well, that's 990 other potential clients I didn't do business with that year. I didn't count it at the time I was a sales agent, but I can safely bet that many of those 990 owners refinanced a building during my relationship with them, and I never even knew about it because I wasn't aware of it at the time and I didn't ask.

A Borrower may ask, "Why do I need you? Money is cheap and plentiful."

And the answer is, "**Well, because you may have certain circumstances in your life or certain issues in your building where the most obvious Lender is not the best Lender for you. There might be another Lender that's better for you. Also, you are making a long-term investment decision, whereas the Lender is making a credit decision, and these are two very different goals. A good *Intermediary* knows how to guide a *Borrower* through the process.**"

Or the shorter version: *"Every property, every owner, and every Lender is different."*

And the only way to know that is by getting into the details and looking at the specifics and doing your analysis.

Hint: You don't want to be part of a hunting trip where you're competing against one or two or three other mortgage brokers out there at the same time. It doesn't do anybody any good. If a Lender sees a loan request from two or three different brokers, the Lender starts to question who's in control. As a result, the Lender will assess the probability of doing a deal to save time. So, they'll pass judgment, ignore your request, or put it on the bottom of the inbox.

Because of this, you want to be the sole broker working with an owner, keeping in mind the owner has to be convinced that you're the right person. You must create, maintain, and communicate your value.

HERE IS THE BLUEPRINT FOR SUCCESS

1. Pick a market area close to where you live.

2. Choose an asset class and or a subclass to focus on. Asset classes include multifamily, retail, office, industrial, or hospitality. Subclasses include senior housing, self-storage, data centers, etc.

3. Determine which CRM system you are comfortable with and what databases contain *owner* names. Databases include Prospect Now and Reonomy.

4. Your goal is to have a database of a *minimum* of 500 owner names. Put them in your CRM.

5. Google all the banks in your market area. Put them in your CRM. Call every bank and ask to speak with the loan officer doing commercial real estate. Make notes and ask if they have a rate sheet they can forward to you.

6. Subscribe to trade publications to read about the market and other general news: *Bisnow, Globestreet, Crittenden, Scottsmans Guide, National Real Estate Investor, CCIM*, etc.

7. Use online listing services like Loopnet and Crexi to learn about the multifamily and investment properties for sale in your market area. Pay attention to the valuations of the properties. Request the broker's setup to study the way a broker prepares the marketing brochure and presents the income and expenses.

8. Collect the names and contact information of the active brokers. Put them in your CRM.

9. If you are focused on multifamily, look up Fannie Mae and Freddie Mac websites. Go to the multifamily section for the latest forms, documents, and information about their programs.

10. Develop a simple script for calling owners.

11. Develop a simple script for calling brokers for referrals.

12. Begin calling.

13. To quote a loan, ask for essential information:

    a. The rent roll

    b. Past 12 months of income and expenses

14. Use the loan sizer Excel spreadsheet to determine the reasonable amount of proceeds a bank will lend. (You will use the metrics discussed later in this book.)

15. Relay information to the Borrower.

16. Once ready to move forward, get a loan application from the Lender and assist the Borrower in collecting all documentation.

17. Submit all documentation to the Lender.

18. The Lender will:

    a. Order the appraisal.

    b. Order the environmental and inspection reports.

    c. Ask for and analyze documents of the Borrower, such as tax returns, property P&Ls for two or three years, current rent rolls, and leases.

    d. Have its loan officer write a credit memo and present to the loan committee.

    e. Committee will approve the loan and provide a Commitment Letter.

19. The Borrower will sign the Commitment Letter.

20. Bank loan documents will be drawn.

21. Borrower signs and, after additional administrative tasks, the loan will fund.

22. Your fee is wired to your company.

NOTES

_____

_____

_____

_____

_____

_____

_____

_____

_____

_____

_____

_____

_____

_____

_____

_____

_____

_____

_____

_____

_____

_____

_____

_____

_____

_____

_____

IDEAL ORIGINATION RELATIONSHIP

Let's discuss the ideal origination process. What I mean by ideal is a **high probability origination process.** If you're new in the business, there can be some confusion as to what a high probability origination process looks like and what a high probability client looks like. *Essentially the Ideal Client is the one who allows you and ONLY YOU to be their representative in the market and who, at some point, signs a Fee Agreement.*

There's an exception to every rule. I have 800 of those stories myself. But given the ideal base case, you're able to better assess whether the other scenarios you find yourself in are going to lead you to a paycheck.

Key Indicators of an Ideal Origination Relationship and How the Process Unfolds

Let's assume you've solicited and met with a client. You've assessed that they have a need, which is to refinance a stabilized asset, such as an apartment building.

First, remember this is the *ideal* situation. You meet with the client. The client expresses to you their motivation. You go through a qualification Q&A with them, and you feel as if you're getting the right answers. You feel as if you understand the motivation. **Key: understanding motivation.** For example, on an apartment building, let's say they had a 10-year agency loan, a Fannie Mae loan. The loan is coming due in March or April and it's now January, and they're looking to refinance.

There's no variability to that loan. It's due and payable. So, their deadline **IS** motivation. You've established they own the building and can make the decision. They've agreed to meet with you. These are all excellent, positive signals. You ask for the appropriate documents, which are the rent roll, the last two years of P&Ls—perhaps you can take last year's P&L on a month-by-month basis. That's really digging in and asking for a lot on the first meeting, but, hey, if they give it to you, you're really passing a lot of tests here. You also want the year-to-date P&L.

You're there, they're talking with you, they give you the documents you need, and, by the way, you have them sign an agreement that says you are their Intermediary, you're their representative in the market, they will not hire anyone else, and if they're solicited by other people, they will direct them to you.

If an asset is *extremely complex* and there's a high mortality rate, for example, in a construction loan origination or a bridge loan origination, *you would almost have to insist on an exclusive or an amended exclusive* because there's a lot of work involved. It can be extremely damaging to your credibility and a big timewaster if a Borrower is using two or more brokers simultaneously or shopping the market themselves without your knowledge.

See Appendix 1.1. Exclusive Fee Agreement on Page 76

Again, this is perfection. It isn't going to be the reality in most cases, but this is the ideal. You're shooting for that exclusive. With that exclusive, you would then have the time and mental space to be able to analyze the numbers, digest the information, and put it into a financing memo.

See Appendix 2. Financing Memo (Examples) on Page 82

If you're new to the business, it is always good to handle this financing memo yourself. Given the specific data and circumstances of the Borrower, you search for the most likely banks and conduct research to learn what Lenders are new to the market, identifying the best Lenders for this opportunity.

Next, you begin to make some calls to Lenders, qualifying their current appetite for the type of opportunity and Borrower you are working on. If you find you have four or five or six interested Lenders, that's great. You would send each of them the financing memo. A well-done memo is a sign of professionalism in the Lender's eyes. **You will not be put onto the bottom of the pile with a good financing memo!**

You can imagine that a Lender has many, many brokers calling them. *Set yourself apart.* If you can provide them with a professionally done memo where you're answering a lot of the questions you know will get asked, they will put you on the top of the list and return your call. They'll be eager to receive deals from you because they know you are organized and prepared.

If you shoot over a rent roll with a wishy-washy message suggesting you're not sure what the client wants, that's a negative impression and harmful to your credibility. You must be prepared.

Following receipt of the financing memo, they'll begin to ask you some questions and they'll provide a *soft quote* or an *indicative quote* which can be verbal or in writing as a term sheet. This is *not* a commitment or a pre-qualification. It is simply an expression of interest.

See Appendix 3. Term Sheet Sample on Page 91

After speaking with Lenders, you will take those quotes and put them in a chart we call a *matrix*—a simple chart that shows and compares the different Lenders, their programs, their pricing, and their terms.

See Appendix 4. Lender Matrix Quotes on Page 93

You sit with the Borrower and provide them the matrix and go through all the Lenders and all the choices. This process accomplishes a couple of things. First, you're testing the motivation of the Borrower. Second, you have demonstrated your professionalism and the Borrower sees that you're working hard and bringing back some great information. This professionalism and hard work help to cement the relationship and your credibility and trustworthiness.

The Borrower will begin to question the specifics.

For example, "Can they maybe soften up on the prepay? Or maybe we can go a little less recourse?" It would be your job to go back and try to negotiate specifics with the Lender.

Once the Borrower is satisfied, you will get an application from the Lender. You might want to fill out some of the necessary information for the Borrower and then either email it to the Borrower or provide it to the Borrower in person and help them through it.

I have found that if a Borrower gets something like an application over email, it's not exactly the most fun thing to dive into. A Borrower only does this every so often, maybe every 5–10 years. So maybe they're a little rusty. **As the Intermediary, you want to help them through this part of the process.**

See Appendix 5. Commercial Loan Application on Page 95

Every Lender, except for maybe 1 out of 20, will require a third-party deposit. The Borrower is paying for the appraisal, or any third party involved. Deliver the completed application and the check to the bank.

So again, that was the core ideal of high probability and what you're looking for in an origination relationship with a Borrower. Naturally, there are variants to that ideal process. I'll mention a couple.

RESOURCES

Access valuable downloads at
www.SilverthreadCapitalU.com

Look for the word **"Appendix"** at the bottom of the website. Click. Create a log-in account and get exclusive access to valuable files.

Variations on the Ideal #1:
Another Quote on the Table

Sometimes a Borrower tells you they already received a verbal quote. I emphasize this situation because if they don't show you the quote and tell you verbally instead, "Well, I have a quote, and it's this," they may be happy with that quote and merely using you to validate that what they have is the best they're going to get.

This happens a lot. You may think you have a lead, so you're working hard to try to beat their original quote. But if you don't know the other quote and **haven't read it for yourself**, you're in a situation where you don't know for sure if the quote is genuine. You don't know anything about it other than the Borrower's saying, "I have a quote for 4.5%. And, boy, if you can beat that, I'll use you."

In some instances, that's fine. You can do that. My first deal was precisely that kind of *"Can you beat this?"* assignment. **But here is the important difference: we asked for and received the other bank's term sheet letter.** We read the letter. We did our market discovery research with our Lenders and determined there was a high probability we could beat the existing quote.

However, there is a risk involved. Sometimes you may go back with your Lender's offer, and the Borrower takes your letter or quote to his current Lender, and they match it. That's happened to me a couple of times. It hurts, but it happens. So again, you have to be careful. Ensure with the Borrower that they will use your services if you can bring a quote that beats the one they currently have. Alternatively, work out a deal where if they go back and make a deal based on your work, maybe you can get paid a little bit of a break fee for your time.

Keep in mind, in many instances, a Borrower who's not in the market frequently confuses a soft quote or an indicative term sheet with a real quote or even a commitment. They think that the indicative quote is precisely what the Lender's going to give them. Reading the terms that they say they have in hand is extremely important.

Time after time, when I read the document, I find issues the Borrower did not see or understand or know why they should care.

Examples of this are recourse versus non-recourse, yield mainte-nance versus step down prepay, loan reset terms at the end of the fixed-rate period, loan-to-value (LTV) rebalances, and others.

One tactic you should consider if a Borrower has an existing quote from a Lender is to get a signed agreement from the client excluding that current Lender. I call it a "'partial exclusive."

The Borrower has nothing to lose. You're taking on an as-signment, the "Can you beat this?" assignment, because you feel that you can beat what he has on the table. If you have a break fee and you're willing to put in the time to build that rela-tionship, and you want to get out there into the market with a "live deal" to talk with Lenders about, you can take that assign-ment on. *It's a calculated business decision.*

Variations on the Ideal #2: Low Probability Situation

On the other end of the spectrum is a low probability situation where you might have a lead from the accountant, the lawyer, or another networking source, and they provide you with all the information but want you to "work it through them." Don't get me wrong, leads are great! But you must talk with the Borrower.

You don't know what's going on there. You don't see the motivation of the Borrower. You don't know the hot buttons. A lot of details go into pursuing one of these loans.

So just having information and running with it without having spoken to the Borrower, either on a "Can you beat this?" assign-ment or an "I know this guy, and he needs a loan" type of *opportunity, is a potential time-wasting time bomb*. You have no agreement with the Borrower. You have no idea of what other quotes they're getting or who else they're using. That is an extremely low probability assignment, and you must be extremely careful not to be tempted to take that on solely for practice.

Also consider that you can lose credibility with your wealth advisor or your lead source. After all, they don't understand the process very well because they're not involved in it daily. They might think you have some magic money somewhere and show up with the best price and terms, and that can be a problem for your credibility.

On the other hand, with the Lenders you're talking to, if you don't have control of the information or in-depth knowledge of the information, you will most certainly lose credibility.

Summary of the Ideal Client and Process:

1. *Know the motivation of the Borrower.*

2. *Get a fee agreement from the Borrower.*

3. *Work referral sources* but *talk directly with the Borrower.*

4. *Do the financing memo yourself to understand the numbers.*

5. *Be prepared to answer questions* you know *the banker will ask.*

6. *Help the Borrower with the loan application.*

7. *Stay involved in the process.*

NOTES

DISCUSSION OF BANKS, NON-BANK LENDERS, AND THE FIVE Cs OF CREDIT

The banking world is opaque. It isn't very transparent to the end user. Our business as Intermediaries is **necessary precisely for that reason.** Sure, people say, "Hey, I can go directly to my bank and get a loan." In many cases, that is true if everything is perfect. *However, in our business, everything is rarely if ever perfect.*

For instance, Borrowers have issues that you really wouldn't know until you get into it with them. For example, banks have specific criteria that they're clear about in the first half of the year. Still, their criteria can change based on volumes they are lending or market-related changes. So many inputs go into making a loan decision, and the average Borrower has *no way* of knowing which Lender is the best for them.

Here are some of the characteristics and things you need to know about Lenders.

Footprint: Local, Regional, Super-regional, and National

Lenders have what's called a footprint: some Lenders will provide loans within their county and only their county. Some Lenders will offer loans in a specified region. The first type of Lender is probably a community bank. The second type of Lender is a regional bank. You might have a super-regional bank that lends only in the Northeast or just the Southeast. Then you have your national and global Lenders like Wells Fargo, Bank of America, Citigroup, and so on.

So those Lender footprints are essential to know because, if you're talking with a Lender on behalf of a client in Westchester County and that client is buying a property in Florida, those Lenders you know in that particular county may not lend on an asset in Florida. You have to go find a Florida bank with a footprint in the area where the property is located that you want to finance. Some Lenders will not lend on what are called special-use properties like hotels, gas stations, self-storage, or healthcare. On the other hand, some Lenders specialize in hotels, gas stations, self-storage, and healthcare. *So getting to know who those Lenders are is part of your value-add for a client.*

How do you find out? Just ask the Lender: "What's your footprint?" and "Can you tell me about your core programs?"

Bankers Can Be Polite but *Not Interested*

You also need to decide if a banker understands the real estate. In many cases, bankers are very polite. They're thinking in the long-term. They don't want to say "no" to anyone. So, a banker might say, "Well, you know, we don't do that, but we'll take a look at it." When you hear a banker say, "We'll take a look at it," he or she is being polite. Honestly, the likelihood of their doing that deal is very slim. Move on. Go find a Lender who's excited to do a special-use property or perhaps a Borrower who might not have the best credit score. Lenders have specific criteria and policies they use to decide to lend; they call it their *credit box*. Some Lenders will make loans from half a million to, let's say, $2 million.

You will learn the various Lenders' credit box criteria during your "market discovery" conversations with them.

Par Pricing

Some banks will have what's called *par pricing*. **In other words, they do not charge a fee**. Other banks will charge a point, which you need to be careful about because we make our living charging the Borrower 1% of the loan amount. If you have a charge of 1%, and the bank also wants to charge 1%, that might be a deal killer. So again, knowing those Lenders who are par Lenders is in your best interest as an Intermediary.

Compensating Balance

Many Lenders, especially the business banks or the community banks, would require what's called a *compensating balance*. In other words, if they lend you $2 million, they want as much as 10% or a compensating balance of $200,000 left in the bank on deposit. In my experience, compensating balances are a nonstarter with a lot of the real estate owners I deal with. You'll find that real estate people like to be cash poor and real estate rich. They want to put that $200,000 to use. They don't want it sitting in a bank account. So, if a bank has a compensating balance, you must know that up-front because if, at the eleventh hour when the Commitment Letter comes through and everything is approved, there's a small paragraph in there that reads, "Oh, by the way, we need to have a compensating balance," that can be a time waster and a deal killer.

Keeping It in Our Bank

Many banks require the operating account of that particular property they're making a loan on. The bank wants the rent coming in deposited and the expense checks being written from the operating account at the bank. However, consider that some owners might have ten properties all banked at the same place. They don't want to start having ten different bank accounts, so that could be a deal killer. Again, this is the information you need to know upfront. It's generally in writing on a term sheet. When it isn't, this is a question that you should be asking the banker when you're interviewing them.

Credit Score

One of the most important metrics a Lender looks at is the Borrower's credit score. A score of 680 is a standard credit benchmark. Most Lenders will go down to 650 if they like the property and the Borrower. A lot of what are called *non-bank Lenders or specialty Lenders* enter the market, and they're lending on properties where the owner might have a credit score of less than 650. Generally, a credit score that goes down to 600 is tolerable by those specialty Lenders.

And in many cases, even the specialty Lenders will turn away deals where a credit score is in the low five hundred range—unless there is a compelling story with documentation to back it up.

Personal Guarantees

Also, most banks require personal guarantees. Some banks are *nonrecourse Lenders*. If you start thinking about it, a nonrecourse loan is significant. The loan doesn't show up on your personal credit file. If something goes wrong, they won't come after your house. Also, having a nonrecourse loan is of extreme importance for many partnerships because, generally speaking, the general partner may only have 10% equity in the deal; yet he's being asked to personally guarantee a loan of $2–5 million dollars. That just doesn't make sense for a lot of general partners. So they would be looking for a nonrecourse loan. Personal guarantees, or PGs, are required by a lot of banks, and it's good to know which ones do not require them.

Borrowers Need Intermediaries

These are the opaque characteristics of Lenders that a lot of Borrowers do not understand. A Borrower who believes that they can save money by not hiring you may choose the wrong bank for any one of the above reasons. Bankers tend to be polite and are willing to serve a client who came directly to them. The banker may have an inkling that the loan request will not make it through the credit process, but they put in the effort to satisfy the client. They write a credit memo to their credit committee, and then they leave it up to their credit committee to say, "No, thank you," all in the effort of trying to service a client.

In many cases, you will hear clients say that they applied for a loan and were turned down after 60 days of providing documents and paying for the inspections and appraisals.

As originators, we work on probability. We need to know some of those traits that I've mentioned about Lenders and to understand their credit box so we know upfront if a Lender is right for a particular client and their specific needs, so we can place the loan with the highest probable Lender.

The Five Cs of Credit: Every Bank Uses These

The five Cs of credit is a system used by Lenders to gauge the creditworthiness of potential Borrowers. The system weighs five characteristics of the Borrower and conditions of the loan, attempting to estimate the chance of default and, consequently, the risk of a financial loss for the Lender. The five Cs of credit are *character*, *capacity*, *capital*, *collateral*, and *conditions*.

1. **Character**—*reflected by the applicant's credit history.*

2. **Capacity**—*the applicant's* **and the property** *debt-to-income ratio.*

3. **Capital**—*the amount of money an applicant has, aka liquidity.*

4. **Collateral**—*an asset that can back or act as security for the loan.*

5. **Conditions**—*the purpose of the loan, the amount involved, and prevailing interest rates.*

NOTES

_____

_____

_____

_____

_____

_____

_____

_____

_____

_____

_____

_____

_____

_____

_____

_____

_____

_____

_____

_____

_____

_____

_____

TYPES OF LOANS

Now that we've discussed some of the characteristics of banks, let's go into the topic of the many types of commercial loans. There will be some crossover information here, but we will put it into more context.

Numerous banks and CMBS Lenders and originators are providing different types of commercial real estate loans, and I wanted just to name them here so you can get a broad understanding of what they're generally about.

Agency Loans

Let's start with an *agency loan*.

Fannie Mae (https://multifamily.fanniemae.com) and Freddie Mac (https://mf.freddiemac.com/product/sbl.html) are two quasi-governmental agencies that are providing financing for multi-family housing.

You don't submit a loan to those agencies. You must go through an approved seller-servicer company like Greystone, Ready Capital, or Arbor that are authorized to underwrite and approve loans according to Fannie and Freddie's standards. They'll make $100 million or $200 million worth of loans and turn around and sell those loans to the agencies.

Agency loans are *nonrecourse*. They're usually for longer-term investors and stabilized assets. You have to have 85–90% occupancy before they would consider funding an agency loan. It's generally for a client who has a stable asset and wants long-term, nonrecourse money at very competitive rates.

Bridge Loans

A bridge loan is a loan that will bridge you from where the property is now, which is usually a less-than-ideal condition, to where you want to get that property. For example, if you wanted an agency loan, it wouldn't be in your best interest to get a long-term, 10-year loan on a property that you could improve within a year and then raise the rent. You probably want to hold off on putting that permanent agency loan on it. You want to wait until you have that property cleaned up and fixed up to raise the rent and earn more proceeds. You might do that with a bridge loan or rehab loan.

It isn't a construction loan. A bridge loan is used if a structure is in place and needs rehabilitation to bring it to its highest and best use. Depending on the location, the experience of the sponsor, and the condition of the property, bridge loan rates can be as low as 4% or as high as 10%.

Also, bridge loans are often used for a quick closing. You may not have the time to go to a Lender to do complete underwriting, and you must act quickly. That's where a bridge loan can come in. This type of loan is commonly known as a *hard money loan.*

Cash-Out Refi

Please note if you have a client who wants to refinance and is seeking to pay off an existing loan with a new mortgage in an amount higher than the current loan, it's called a cash-out refi. The reason I want to include it here is that the agency Lenders, the bridge Lenders, or CMBS Lenders will generally accept a cash-out refi, but they want to know why. What is the sponsor (Borrower) going to be doing with the money? It's useful to understand these things if you're talking with a Lender for a Borrower who wants more money than the senior debt currently on the property. For instance, let's say you have a $2 million loan presently on a property, and the property net income can support a larger loan say $3MM. If the Borrower requests a new loan of $3 million and will settle for anything over the current loan of $2MM, that's called a cash-out refi. When you approach your Lenders, you should let them know that upfront.

Cash-In Refi

A cash-in refi is just the opposite. *You might have a situation where a very conservative Borrower wants to pay his loan down. Or, the value of the property has come down, and you have to cut a check to refinance the property.* I recently had a call from a New York City investor who had a $20 million loan on a property located in Times Square in NYC. The value of the property decreased because his leases were not renewing, and some other complicating factors came into play. The bank re-appraised the asset and decided to reduce their exposure. They calculated a $17 million loan was the maximum senior loan exposure for the asset. Common in loan documents is language enabling a bank the ability to request a payoff of the $20 million should the LTV be "out of balance."

When we analyzed the asset for the owner, it turned out that the largest loan we could get on that property would be about $17 million. He would have to write a check for $3 million and do a cash-in refi. Generally, in a declining market, you will see cash-in refis.

Construction Loans

Construction loans are a first mortgage where the proceeds are used to build a structure. Generally, construction loans are not funded 100% day one. Funds are disbursed over time as needed; these disbursements are known as construction draws. Not every Lender does construction loans because of the specialized nature of the relationship, such as reviewing plans and budgets and keeping tabs on the progress and of the builder and timely and frequent disbursement of funds. Most construction loans in the middle market (smaller $1–40 million) are recourse (personally guaranteed) loans. Construction loans are generally excellent business opportunities for an Intermediary because there's always a deadline; a developer has their entitlements and permits, and the clock is ticking.

CMBS Loans

CMBS stands for *commercial mortgage-backed securities*. You might hear people refer to them as *conduit loans*. A CMBS loan is where a Wall Street bank is originating loans to then make into securities to sell to an institutional investor. Let's say it's a $250 million pool of mortgages. There might be 25 or 50 properties in that pool. They will then turn around and make those streams of income into bonds, and they will sell the mortgage to institutions as a bond investment versus a direct real estate investment.

I'm not going to get into how they slice and dice the different yield categories, but you ought to know that it's called *tranches*. They provide, for example, the most secure AAA income stream or less safe B pieces. Some investors prefer lower risk AAA and lower yields, whereas others are willing to take on more risk, and they'll buy the lower grade bonds with a higher return. You can link here for a more in-depth explanation: <u>More CMBS Details here.</u>[1]

CMBS loans are non-recourse—except for standard *carve-outs*—and generally have 10-year terms. The rates are competitive, and the investment banks are hungry for them. That's how they make their fees: by packaging these loans and then securitizing them. It's always a good relationship and a good conversation I have with my conduit and CMBS Lenders. I enjoy dealing with them.

Fix and Flip Loan

A fix and flip loan is typical in the single-family residential markets. You don't hear that phrase much in the commercial real estate market. Fix and flips are straightforward. Buy a property with borrowed money or buy it all cash and get a fix and flip loan to clean it up, fix it up, and then sell it within a year to flip it out.

Rate and Term Refi

Another term you should know is the *rate and term* refi. Like a cash-out, you should let your Lender know upfront. Lenders like rate and term refis because they're not providing cash out. A rate in term refi means you're providing the Borrower with the same amount of proceeds in the new loan as exists on the current balance of the old loan. A Borrower is refinancing the existing loan because it is due and payable or perhaps interest rates have fallen below his current rate.

---

[1] https://www.reonomy.com/blog/post/cmbs-loans-explained

SBA Loans

I think everybody in this business has heard of an SBA loan. There are two types, a 504 and a 7A. SBA loans are great if you're an owner looking to buy your building or you have a franchise. SBA loans are something you can quickly learn more about on the <u>SBA</u>[2] site. Or see this site: <u>Compare SBA loans 7a vs. 504</u>.[3]

Take-Out Loan, also Known as Permanent Loan

If you have a construction loan that is coming due and the building has been completed, or you have a bridge loan that's coming due and the rehab is complete, you want to remove that construction or that bridge loan. You want to take it out with a permanent mortgage. A *take-out* could be called either a permanent loan or a term loan, where again, you're looking to put a five, seven, or 10-year loan on that property, now that it's complete and stabilized.

---

[2] https://www.sba.gov/category/lender-navigation/sba-loan-programs/7a-loan-programs

[3] https://cdcloans.com/lender/504-7a-loan-comparison/

NOTES

_____

_____

_____

_____

_____

_____

_____

_____

_____

_____

_____

_____

_____

_____

_____

_____

_____

_____

_____

_____

_____

_____

_____

_____

UNDERSTANDING A LENDER'S CREDIT POLICY REQUIREMENTS[4]

With a better understanding of loan types, it now makes sense to dive deeper into the credit policies of Lenders.

When trying to finance a real estate project, it's common for a Borrower to approach multiple Lenders for a loan. Unfortunately, it's equally as common for those same Lenders to provide inconsistent responses. One Lender may look at an opportunity and want nothing to do with it, while another may look at the same opportunity and be quick to approve it. Why?

The answer to this question rests within a lengthy and complex technical document called the *Credit Policy*.

What Is a Credit Policy?

A Lender's Credit Policy is a document that outlines the requirements and procedures for approving a loan. It's the guiding force behind the credit officer's approval or denial decision. The criteria may vary significantly from one Lender to another, which explains the inconsistency. It's rare for anyone outside of a bank or Lender's office to see the Credit Policy.

---

[4] See https://propertymetrics.com/blog/credit-policy/

To demystify the Credit Policy, let's discuss how it gets written, what's in it, and who has the responsibility for maintaining it.

How a Credit Policy Is Written

It's important to note that a credit department's purpose inside of a bank is to analyze new loan and renewal requests and to approve the requests that represent an acceptable level of risk for the bank. It makes sense that there are a series of rules and requirements to govern the entire analysis and credit approval process, which is why the Credit Policy gets created in the first place.

A bank's Credit Policy is created as part of its funding process and with input from the senior executives responsible for managing the bank's risk profile. It's often adapted from another bank or Lender's policy and must be written within regulatory guidelines and formally approved by senior management prior to making the first loan. The actual writing of the policy is a collaborative effort among senior members of the credit department.

What Information Does a Credit Policy Contain?

Specifically, a bank's Credit Policy contains details on three key components of the lending process.

- **Underwriting standards**: The primary function of the document is to define the credit department's underwriting and risk mitigation standards, which includes things like:
  - Identifying characteristics of desirable and undesirable loans
  - Portfolio concentration limits and sub-limits for each loan type

- o Credit approval authority and the approval process
- o The role of the board of directors in reviewing and approving loan requests
- o Financial statement requirements
- o Credit and collateral file maintenance standards
- o Guidelines for appraisal practices

- **Elements of an acceptable Credit Memo:** The details of an individual loan request are written up in a document called a *Credit Memo,* and the Credit Policy outlines the elements of an acceptable memo, including:
  - o Loan purpose
  - o Sources of repayment
  - o Collateral description and valuation
  - o Analysis of Borrower and guarantor financial condition
  - o Risk
  - o Identification of any Credit Policy exceptions

- **Credit risk management and monitoring procedures:** Once the loan is made, the Credit Policy also outlines the procedures for ensuring that the deal remains an acceptable level of risk to the bank. This includes things such as the following:
  - o Elements of an effective loan review system, including frequency, scope, and depth
  - o Requirements for an effective credit grading system
  - o Portfolio mix and risk diversification guidelines
  - o Collection and problem loan resolution procedures

    o   Methodology for establishing sufficient allowance for loan losses

    o   Procedures to identify, approve, and monitor all Credit Policy exceptions

Credit Policy Example

For Borrowers, the most mysterious and confusing part of a Lender's Credit Policy is the approval criteria. This is often the portion of the policy that may vary the most from one Lender to another. As such, let's look at an example of the approval criteria for a multifamily loan from a regional bank's actual Credit Policy:

Criteria	Normal Policy	"In The Box"
LTV / LTC	Max LTV = 80%, Max LTC = 100%	Max LTV = 80%, Max LTC = 85%
DSC Ratio	1.25X	1.25X
Amortization	N/A	25–30 Years
Underwriting Rate	N/A	7.50% Floor
Vacancy Assumption	N/A	5% – 7%
Term	10–20 Years	10–20 Years
Recourse	100% Unconditional	100% Unconditional
Project Size	N/A	350+ Units
Expenses	N/A	>30% EGI
Reserves	N/A	$250 Per Unit, Per Year

From the table, there are relatively few defined policy criteria: 80% Loan to Value, 1.25X Debt Service Coverage, and 10–20 years term. Let's call these the "formal" criteria. "Formal" criteria seldom change.

However, a bank may also have informal criteria, which may be referred to as their "risk appetite" or "in the box" criteria. This is what is likely to change in response to market fluctuations and portfolio concentrations. They're also at the root of why one bank may want to do a deal, and another may want nothing to do with it.

Ask About the "Appetite"

As a best practice, it's usually a good idea to ask a bank or Lender upfront if they have "appetite" for your deal type. If they don't, there's no sense in forcing the issue. It's best to move on to another Lender.

NOTES

DSCR AND DEBT YIELD

Having covered types of banks, types of loans, and some of the intricacies involved, let's look at some of the methods banks use to quantify the amount of a mortgage they are willing to give.

DSCR

Let's go into the *debt coverage ratio* first. This is often written as the acronym DCR. Some people call it a "debt service coverage ratio," or DSCR, and I'll also mention something called debt yield. However, a debt coverage ratio is quite simply a ratio or a comparison of the amount of net income on a property versus the mortgage payments, also known as debt service (DS).

Contrast a home loan with an income property loan. In a home mortgage, a Lender will look at the income of the Borrower from all sources to see whether or not they can afford the loan on the house they're buying. The debt to income ratio of the potential homeowner is the key metric. In the income property business, a Lender will look at the income from a property and *only* the income from a property. **That property must stand alone on its own merits, and the property income must support the loan payments—debt service, also known as mortgage payments—due each month.**

It's worth mentioning that one of the confusing issues *for a new buyer* of an income property is the loan-to-value versus debt-service-coverage-ratio calculation to determine the size of a loan. You will always hear and see in writing a Lender advertising, "We'll lend up to 75% loan to value." So, if a property is listed for sale for $1 million, some new buyers will say, "Awesome, I'll be able to get a $750,000 loan, and I can come in with $250,000 and buy that building." Then what happens is, once we start looking at the income, maybe the building is being sold for $1 million, but the net income before debt service can support a loan of only $500,000. So, the buyer would have to then come in with $500,000 in cash to purchase the property.

You need to know that up front, and it's relatively easy math to calculate. The debt coverage ratio is important to know because, in some A areas, a debt coverage ratio will be lower than in some C or D areas where the debt coverage ratio will be higher.

Again, a *debt coverage ratio* is the comparison of the debt service versus the net operating income of the property. For instance, if a Lender requires 1.25 DSCR to make a loan, and let's just say the mortgage payment in the first year is $1, you would have to have $1.25 of net income to *cover* the mortgage payment.

If, for example, it's a property in a C or D area, a Lender wants to be more conservative. They would say we need to have a debt coverage ratio of 1.5. So the property would have to have a net operating income of $1.50 to the $1 of debt service (mortgage payment) on that property.

It's a quick ratio used in calculating the size of loans. We'll get into that in another chapter, where I'll show you how to calculate a loan using a debt coverage ratio as one of the data points to determine the size of a loan.

RESOURCES

See the section called "Let's Do the Math"
on Page 51 to learn more about how to size a loan.

Debt Yield

I also want to mention debt yield. Debt yield is even simpler. A Lender might say, "I'm going to lend you money, and you know what? If you happen to lose that property for whatever reason and I need to repossess it, I want to know that the net income on that property is going to give me a good return for my risk. I don't want to lose money by lending you money, so if I have to repossess that property and suddenly I'm the banker, and I own it, I need to know that I'm yielding a certain amount of money, a certain percentage every year, if I own that property."

Let's just say once again, hypothetically, that a property is throwing off net income of $100,000 a year and I gave you a loan of $1 million. If I were to take that property back, the net income would provide me with a 10% yield on my money: $100,000 divided by my $1,000,000 loan.

Lenders look at loans, and they might say, "I require a 10 debt yield on my money."

So you go to them and you say, "Hey, I need a loan on XYZ property. How much of a loan can you give me?"

Without doing any calculation at all, within a matter of seconds, the Lender will say, "Well, what's the net income?"

You'll say, "Well, it's $100,000," and the Lender might say, "I'll lend you $1 million."

That's a 10 debt yield.

Debt yield is a fast way for a Lender and a Borrower to assess whether or not they want to work together.

NOTES

PREPAY PENALTIES

Most loans have prepayment penalties. The rationale is that the Lender wants to make a consistent yield on the money they lend over a fixed period of time. Lenders do not want to churn loans. So a prepayment penalty is a way to discourage payoffs and to maintain a predictable yield.

In commercial real estate, there are two or three types of prepayment penalties. One is called a declining or *step-down prepay*. Another is called *yield maintenance*. Another is *defeasance*, which is most common in the CMBS world. There's also a concept known as *lockout*, which allows a prepay only following a set duration.

Step-Down Prepay

A *step-down prepay*, or *declining prepay*, is generally tied to the fixed duration of a loan.

For instance, if the fixed term is five years, you may see a prepay stated like so: "5, 4, 3, 2, 1." Some Lenders might have 5% for the first two years, and then 1%, 1%, 1% for the last three years. It just depends on what the Lender publishes and what you can negotiate.

So "5, 4, 3, 2, 1" on a five-year term would mean that you would multiply the amount of the loan by 5% if you were to prepay that loan off in the first year of the life of that loan; and it declines from there. In the last year of the loan, you would have a 1% prepay, and at the end of the fixed term, you would have zero prepay penalties.

Some loans, following the fixed duration of the loan, revert to an adjustable rate. Still, there'd be no prepay, so you'd be able to get another loan to pay off the current mortgage if you didn't want to be subject to the vagaries of the market with an adjustable-rate loan.

Yield Maintenance

Yield Maintenance is a guarantee of the yield to the Lender or the buyer of the mortgage. An institution is making a loan, and that institution doesn't want to be in the business of churning loans. They want to have it on their books with a fixed and steady yield. If prepaid, they want to maintain the yield expected. The calculation of the penalty is a present-value calculation. The Borrower who prepays a loan with yield maintenance would be required to pay a lump sum based on the formula in the prepayment language of the loan documents. A more detailed view is available here: <u>Yield Maintenance.</u>[5]

Defeasance

Most CMBS loans will have yield maintenance or *defeasance* prepays. If you look up defeasance, it's a concept that comes out of the bond world. Keep in mind commercial mortgage-backed securities are bonds. So if you wanted to pay off the loan, what you'd be doing is defeasing the bonds, which means that you're replacing the bonds that you're paying off with another set of bonds that the institutional investor can then draw a yield from. The cost of doing that, in the first few years of a CMBS loan, is

---

[5] https://www.investopedia.com/terms/y/yieldmaintenance.asp

generally very, very prohibitive. This is just a generality, but as a percentage, defeasance costs end up being higher than 10% in the first several years of the loan. So, it's rarely used unless there's an excellent reason for it. A more detailed view is available here: Defeasance.[6]

Be Prepared for Prepay

The prepay issue almost always comes up. **If a Borrower is looking to harvest money from their real estate portfolios periodically, the prepay can become a deal killer.** So, it's worth it to you as an Intermediary to understand upfront the motivations of the Borrower and the various Lenders' prepay language and how to negotiate better prepays.

---

[6] https://www.investopedia.com/terms/d/defeasance.asp

NOTES

LET'S DO THE MATH

Note: watching the video is a good idea for this section.

RESOURCES

I suggest you watch the instructional video and download the Loan Sizer Spreadsheet from the Silverthread Capital University website at

www.SilverthreadCapitalU.com

Look for the word **"Appendix"** at the bottom of the Website. Click. Create log-in account and get exclusive access to valuable files.

Let's do some math—we're going to "size up a loan." We're going to determine the proceeds or the size of a loan based on the net operating income of a property. We've put together a spreadsheet you can download and play around with, learning as you go. It's what we use to size up a loan, and it's what we use to send over to Lenders to show them we've done our work, which they appreciate. They see that we've done a lot of the work for them, so it's well received.

So let's assume we have qualified a client. They have a need: They own a building, and they want to refinance that property. It's in decent shape and average condition. We don't know anything about the Borrower's credit history. We're just going on face value, based on the information provided to us by the Borrower.

We have on this rent-roll 10 units, including a description and the tenant name, the move-in date, the length of the lease, the total square footage, security deposit, the current rent, if any other charges, for example, garage rent, and then the total current rent.

It's important for Lenders to see when leases were signed. They want to see the duration of the tenant and if there's been a lot of turnover in the property.

Lenders also want to see a description of the unit. In other words: two bed/two bath, one bed/one bath, etc. This helps them to get an idea of what's being charged and, comparatively speaking, if the rents are under or over market.

For simplicity, we have put in $1,000 a month per unit for a total of $10,000 a month, or $120,000 per year in gross annual income. The $120,000 top-line is called *Scheduled Gross Income* (SGI). You should know that even if, let's say, unit #1 is a manager, and they're not paying any rent because they have free rent, we will count that income as the SGI.

So, the SGI is the best-case scenario for that apartment building rental top-line. Even if you had a vacant unit, we would show the scheduled rent for that vacancy that you believe would be attributable to that unit. So it's what the building looks like at 100% occupied.

It's important to note that this is why we want to see a rent roll from an owner. Frequently there are cases where the property has two vacant units and the Borrower tells you (over the phone) their income was $8,000 a month. If you decided to use that number to determine the SGI and then take a common vacancy factor of 5%, you'd be inaccurately calculating the Effective Gross and Net Income. So, be careful *not to double-count* vacancy.

A	B	C	D	E	F	G	H	I	J
Total Potential Gross Income			$8.00	$12,000	$120,000		$8.00	$12,000	$120,000
Less Vacancy (Underwriting)		5.0%	$0.40	$600	$6,000				
Effective Gross Income			$7.60	$11,400	$114,000		$8.00	$12,000	$120,000
Expenses									
Utilities			$0.33	$500	$5,000		$0.00	$0	$0
Insurance			$0.10	$150	$1,500		$0.00	$0	$0
Repairs		5.0%	$0.20	$300	$3,000		$0.20	$300	$3,000
Gardening			$0.33	$500	$5,000		$0.33	$500	$5,000
Cleaning & Maintenance			$0.33	$500	$5,000		$0.33	$500	$5,000
Property Taxes			$0.67	$1,000	$10,000		$0.67	$1,000	$10,000
Misc			$0.33	$500	$5,000		$0.33	$500	$5,000
Other			$0.07	$100	$1,000		$0.07	$100	$1,000
Legal Fees			$0.07	$100	$1,000		$0.07	$100	$1,000
Management Fee		5.0%	$0.40	$600	$6,000		$0.40	$600	$6,000
Total Operating Expenses			$2.83	$4,250	$42,500		$2.40	$3,600	$36,000
Operating Expense Ratio					37.28%				30.00%
Net Operating Income (NOI)			$4.77	$7,150	$71,500		$5.60	$8,400	$84,000
Capital Expenditures									

We use historical operating numbers because we want to show the Lender the past performance of this property. Now again, if you're just doing a quick analysis, you might not have the last two or three years of income and expenses. So, let's just stay focused on 2020, and what we're looking at here is a total rental top line of $120,000.

Let's say there's zero other income, which gives us the total rent of $120,000. There's a 5% vacancy rate. We have the formula baked in here at $6,000, which gives us the Effective Gross Income, the EGI, of $114,000.

I've highlighted what you should be getting from the client. Utilities, insurance, property taxes, management fees, repairs and any major capital improvements (not counted in operating expenses) are the line items to be collected from the client. You can ask for their Schedule E of their Tax returns; but keep in mind many of the expenses can be inflated on the Schedule E. It's always smart to have a conversation with the client to set their mind at ease that you are preparing the analysis and *not* being intrusive or sharing the numbers with anyone. You should also determine which line item expenses are high and adjust for typical operating expenses.

We also need to calculate the cost of landscaping, cleaning, and maintenance. Depending on how much turnover there is in the building, the cleaning and maintenance can be lumped in some cases with repairs. So again, you must look at the books and records of the owner to look at it historically and determine what that figure truly is.

Property taxes are documented and easily calculated.

Miscellaneous could be anything from their auto to their cell phone to meals and entertainment and then legal fees.

Then there's the management fee, which is generally 5% of the gross income, which was $120,000 times 5%, which brings us to $6,000 per year.

11	**Total Potential Gross Income**		$8.00	$12,000	$120,000
13	Less Vacancy (Underwriting)	5.0%	$0.40	$600	$6,000
15	**Effective Gross Income**		$7.60	$11,400	$114,000
17	Expenses				
18	Utilities		$0.33	$500	$5,000
19	Insurance		$0.10	$150	$1,500
20	Repairs	5.0%	$0.20	$300	$3,000
21	Gardening		$0.33	$500	$5,000
22	Cleaning & Maintenance		$0.20	$300	$3,000
23	Property Taxes		$0.67	$1,000	$10,000
24	Misc		$0.33	$500	$5,000
25	Other		$0.07	$100	$1,000
26	Legal Fees		$0.07	$100	$1,000
27	Management Fee	5.0%	$0.40	$600	$6,000
28					
29	**Total Operating Expenses**		$2.70	$4,050	$40,500
30	Operating Expense Ratio				35.53%
31	**Net Operating Income (NOI)**		$4.90	$7,350	$73,500
33	**Capital Expenditures**				
34					

Loan Analysis   Pro Forma   Historicals   Current Rent Roll

Ready

I've seen, in the many apartment buildings that we've done, banks are underwriting 5% vacancy and anywhere from 30–35% expenses, and it just always seems to come out that way.

So now, we have a net operating income of $73,500, and this the number is used to determine the size of the loan, along with other data points, as we discussed in the debt service coverage ratio lesson.

Now, remember, it's $120,000 of gross scheduled income. That's assuming every unit is rented. If, for example, you're paying a manager in the form of a free apartment, you would still count the full rent and then you would bake into the management number that $1,000 a month for the apartment. So the management fee wouldn't be $6,000. This might be a third party management fee or your bookkeeper or some other person who's doing the paperwork, evictions, or whatever. Thus, your management fee could be 5% plus the $12,000 the free apartment accounts for; so that might be a management fee of a total of $18,000 per year. Keep that in mind. If, for example, you have a relative living in the building and the rents are below market, you'd want to make a footnote of that as well.

The Net Operating Income is $73,500, which now rolls into our loan analysis page. You see it here; we've got the $73,500 that comes from the prior calculation. We'd have to know a little bit about the market cap rates because it's going to play into the valuation. The property valuation will play into loan-to-value. If you look on LoopNet[7] or any brokerage site that can provide current for-sale properties in your area, you'll get a feel for the level of CAP rates.

So let's just say, in this area that we're looking at, cap rates are 6%. The approximate value of the property is calculated by taking $73,500, divided by 6%, and you get an estimated market value of $1,225,000.

		Current
Valuation Information		
Net Operating Income (after reserves)	$	73,500
Capitalization Rate		6.00%
Approximate Market Value per Cap Rate		$1,225,000
Price Per Unit		$122,500
Price Per Square Foot		$82
Owner's Equity		$327,136
Loan Analysis		
Loan Request		$897,864
Loan Request Per Unit		$89,786
Underwriting Interest Rate		4.17%

The owner has equity of $327,000, which is the difference between the loan amount and the market value. The owner's equity figure is rarely ever used, but it's kind of nice to see. Also, if you have a buyer who's kicking tires, you can use this to size up a

---

[7] https://www.loopnet.com

loan and then determine how much equity they need to bring to the table as a down payment. So that's how we use this owner equity number.

Owner's Equity	$327,136
Loan Analysis	
Loan Request	$897,864
Loan Request Per Unit	$89,786
Underwriting Interest Rate	4.17%
Term	3 -Years
Amortization	30 -Years
Annual Debt Service	$52,500
Monthly Debt Service	$4,375
Ratios	
Debt Service Coverage Ratio	1.40x
Loan-To-Value	73%
Debt Yield	8.19%

We need to know three things from the bank: the interest rate they're using to size up a loan, the amortization they're using (it could be either 20, 25, or 30), and the debt service coverage ratio they will be using.

The "sizing" formula is baked into this Excel spreadsheet. Once we figure out the *Net Operating Income* (NOI), we would then look at our debt coverage ratio and put in whatever the bank wants. For example, let's say we know that apartment buildings are 1.25 debt coverage ratio. Now, as I've discussed in the DSCR section, that means that for every $1.00 of mortgage, we need $1.25 of net operating income. So, if we put 1.25 in here, it shows that the net income on this property, given a 1.25 debt cover, can support a loan request of $1,005,607.

Approximate Market Value per Cap Rate	**$1,225,000**
Price Per Unit	$122,500
Price Per Square Foot	$82
Owner's Equity	$219,393
Loan Analysis	
Loan Request	$1,005,607
Loan Request Per Unit	$100,561
Underwriting Interest Rate	4.17%
Term	3 -Years
Amortization	30 -Years
Annual Debt Service	$58,800
Monthly Debt Service	$4,900
Ratios	
Debt Service Coverage Ratio	1.25x
Loan-To-Value	82%
Debt Yield	7.31%
Property Analysis	
Units	10

The only problem with that is the loan-to-value pops up to 82%, so it's the loan request here, divided by the value of the property.

That just isn't going to work for most Lenders. An 82% loan-to-value is just a little bit too high. When you're bumping up against the loan-to-value ceiling, it's called loan-to-value *constrained*. Most Lenders are at 75%. As a footnote, some of the agency Lenders will go to 80% on an acquisition.

So if you're bumping up against an 82% LTV, you need to adjust the DSCR. So let's go 1.35 DSCR, and you're at 76% LTV.

So let's go 1.37 DSCR, and you're at 75% right on the nose. 75% will fit most Lenders' credit boxes and this interest rate.

Underwriting Interest Rate	4.17%
Term	3 -Years
Amortization	30 -Years
Annual Debt Service	$53,650
Monthly Debt Service	$4,471
Ratios	
Debt Service Coverage Ratio	1.37x
Loan-To-Value	75%
Debt Yield	8.01%
Property Analysis	
Units	10
Rentable Area	15,000 SF
Avg. Rents PSF/YR	$8.00
Expenses PSF/YR	$2.70
Expenses Per Unit/YR	$4,050
Expense Ratio (Total Expenses/EGI)	35.53%

Let's see how the loan changes. Hypothetically, if we want to go for a three-year loan and amortize it over 30 years, and let's say today we can get a rate of 3.5%, we'll see how this loan amount changes to $995K.

Valuation Information		
Net Operating Income (after reserves)	$	73,500
Capitalization Rate		6.00%
Approximate Market Value per Cap Rate		$1,225,000
Price Per Unit		$122,500
Price Per Square Foot		$82
Owner's Equity		$229,375
Loan Analysis		
Loan Request		$995,625
Loan Request Per Unit		$99,563
Underwriting Interest Rate		3.50%
Term		3 -Years
Amortization		30 -Years
Annual Debt Service		$53,650
Monthly Debt Service		$4,471

Please note that if your amortization changes, the loan amount will be impacted. An apartment building in Houston, Texas, versus one in Los Angeles, California will have 25-year amortization versus 30-year amortization, thus impacting loan proceeds.

So if in Houston, a bank useses a 25-year amortization, we change the figure and see how that loan amount changes here to 893K.

Valuation Information		
Net Operating Income (after reserves)	$	73,500
Capitalization Rate		6.00%
Approximate Market Value per Cap Rate		$1,225,000
Price Per Unit		$122,500
Price Per Square Foot		$82
Owner's Equity		$331,953
Loan Analysis		
Loan Request		$893,047
Loan Request Per Unit		$89,305
Underwriting Interest Rate		3.50%
Term		3 -Years
Amortization		25 -Years
Annual Debt Service		$53,650
Monthly Debt Service		$4,471

So here we see the amortization, the interest rate that the bank is using to underwrite or analyze the property, and the debt service coverage ratio, the data points, and the metrics that are used to determine the size of the loan. This is a handy calculator for that.

It's just the NOI divided by the size of the loan that gives you your percentage yield or debt yield. We said it was 10 units, 15,000 feet. All these averages are baked into this and done for you.

Term	3 -Years
Amortization	25 -Years
Annual Debt Service	$53,650
Monthly Debt Service	$4,471

Ratios

Debt Service Coverage Ratio	1.37x
Loan-To-Value	73%
Debt Yield	8.23%

Property Analysis

Units	10
Rentable Area	15,000 SF
Avg. Rents PSF/YR	$8.00
Expenses PSF/YR	$2.70
Expenses Per Unit/YR	$4,050
Expense Ratio (Total Expenses/EGI)	35.53%

If an Excel sheet is unavailable, you can size up a loan on a financial calculator like an HP 12C; that's a Hewlett-Packard 12C, which you can buy for $60 or download for $4.99 on your phone or your iPad.

If you want to use an Excel spreadsheet, we baked in all these numbers using our Excel formulas, and you'd have to go to the equation on the financial formulas tab, and the present value (PV) formula. We standardized this Excel sheet for your use.

Metrics for Loan Amount (DO NOT CHANGE)	
0.29%	RATE
300	NPER
(4,471)	PMT

So if you're using, for example, as I have here, 3.50 divided by 12, that's 0.29% a month. So let's just say, hypothetically, it's 12%; you can see monthly it's 1%, right?

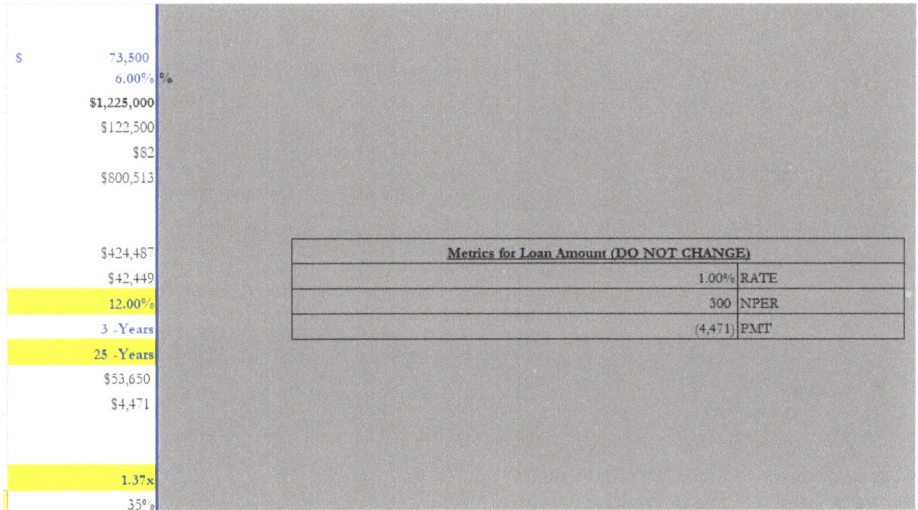

		$	73,500	
			6.00%	%
		$1,225,000		
		$122,500		
		$82		
		$800,513		

	Metrics for Loan Amount (DO NOT CHANGE)	
$424,487		
$42,449	1.00%	RATE
12.00%	300	NPER
3 -Years	(4,471)	PMT
25 -Years		
$53,650		
$4,471		
1.37x		
35%		

So you'll have loans that are going to be at 4%, let's say; your monthly rate is 0.33.

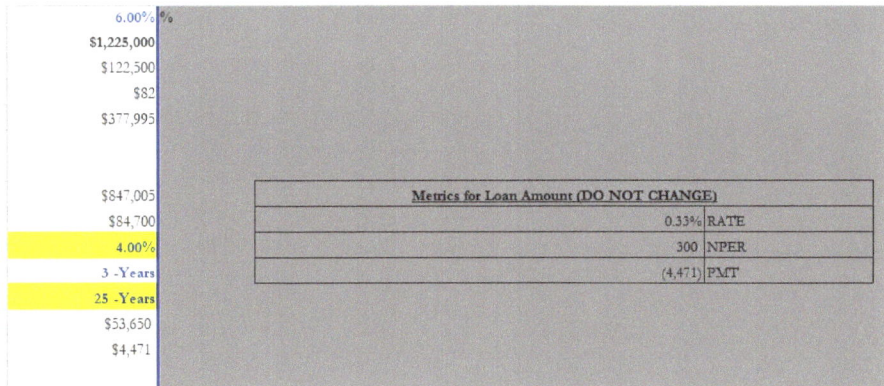

		6.00%	%
$1,225,000		
$122,500		
$82		
$377,995		

	Metrics for Loan Amount (DO NOT CHANGE)	
$847,005		
$84,700	0.33%	RATE
4.00%	300	NPER
3 -Years	(4,471)	PMT
25 -Years		
$53,650		
$4,471		

The amortization is right here. For amortization, it says NP, which is the number of periods that the loan purportedly will be paid back. So let's change the amortization. You'll see most amortizations for apartment buildings are at 30 years, so your amortization is 360 months.

And then the payment (PMT) will be your NOI divided by your debt service coverage ratio. So your payment is your net operating income divided by your debt service coverage ratio.

So, let's say your debt service coverage ratio is 2; that means, for every $1 of mortgage payments, you need $2 of income. You'll see how your loan is going to go down to $641,000, so correspondingly, your loan payment is lower.

Capitalization Rate	6.00%
Approximate Market Value per Cap Rate	$1,225,000
Price Per Unit	$122,500
Price Per Square Foot	$82
Owner's Equity	$583,525

Loan Analysis

		Metrics for Loan Amount (DO NOT CHANGE)	
Loan Request	$641,475		
Loan Request Per Unit	$64,148	0.33%	RATE
Underwriting Interest Rate	4.00%	360	NPER
Term	3 - Years	(3,063)	PMT
Amortization	30 - Years		
Annual Debt Service	$36,750		
Monthly Debt Service	$3,063		

Ratios

Debt Service Coverage Ratio	2.00x
Loan-To-Value	52%
Debt Yield	11.46%

So a loan payment going lower could be a good thing if you have enough equity to put down as a down payment. You'll see here, in some excellent properties, let's say **AAA** tenants are in there, you might have a 1.05 debt coverage ratio and your loan value pops up to $1,221,000, so that formula again is under formulas, financial, PV. It's a present-value formula. Just remember that everything must be by month.

Keep in mind that every property, from apartment buildings to hotels, across the board, is done the same way. It's always drilling down to the net operating income and then determining what debt coverage ratio a Lender is using for that particular asset class, the amortization they're using for that asset class, and the interest rate being used at any given point on the timeline.

So those are the things you need to learn. It isn't that hard. Once you do the first one, you'll see that every other asset class is precisely the same process. As you can see, for those of you who might be or have been in the single-family residential business, it's a heck of a lot different than the way a loan size is determined for the purchase of a house.

NOTES

COMPETITION TYPES

Let's cover the competitive landscape. A lot of people refer to the brokerage shops as "platforms." There are different types of platforms and business models, which I will discuss here, so you know what to expect if you're looking for a position at one of these companies or you're competing against one of them. There are some pluses and minuses, and some not-so-apparent scenarios you should know. With these in mind, you'll be better prepared to approach the business with your eyes open.

Pure-Play Commercial Real Estate Mortgage Brokerage Shop

The first platform I'd like to discuss is what's called a "pure-play commercial real estate mortgage brokerage shop." *For example, Silverthread Capital is not owned by a bank and not owned or embedded in a commercial real estate brokerage shop or a residential real estate brokerage shop. There's one main advantage: We're able to solicit business from brokers from different brokerage shops.* As a result, we get a lot of business from commercial real estate brokers. If we were embedded in a brokerage company, we would be limited to doing business with those agents. You can imagine how awkward it would be carrying a card of a brokerage company and soliciting business in another brokerage company. I know firsthand that it's very, very difficult to walk into another brokerage company and say, "Hey, we don't share information with the sale brokers or the leasing brokers; we're sort of a different division." That's not going to happen.

What about being the in-house Intermediary at a commercial real estate company? That sounds great, but unless you have trust with those other people that you're trying to solicit business from, it's a challenging way to get business. And so we see another one of the downsides here. Imagine you're in one of those shops and for whatever reason, you're not producing. This might be because the leads aren't coming through that shop; maybe the folks in that shop are using your buddy at the next desk since they've known him or her for longer than you; or the type of business they're doing is just not the kind of business you want to be doing. For example, maybe that company's doing only small deals or perhaps they're doing just the deals that are too big for what you want to focus on. As you can see, there are lots of different things you need to look at if you're going to join a platform that's embedded in another larger real estate brokerage company.

The upside, of course, is if you become one of the top producers, you will typically be very successful. And in sales, this is somewhat the truth: There's an 80/20 dynamic going on where 20% of the personnel produce 80% of the results. The ratio could be a little bit different, but you'll always find there are star performers in every sales organization. If there are 10 mortgage originators in one of those embedded shops, you can bet that 2 or 3 or maybe 4 of them are the top earners because they have somehow succeeded, whether it is through sheer competence, perhaps nepotism, perhaps old boy network, or whatever reason.

I know that sounds negative, but this is the reality of it. To be fair, I did lead off with saying pure competence can win the day, which is especially true over time and after you build trust. And if you're new in that shop, it's going to be very, very difficult for you. It might take two years for you to pop through and start doing deals on a flow basis. You need to be aware of that if you're starting out. Of course, if you're not just starting out, and if you have a book of business and you're moving over to that other brokerage company, well then fine, then that is irrelevant for you. Fortunately, if that were true, you would probably not be reading this book.

Correspondent Shop

The next type of competitor I'd like to mention is what's called a "correspondent shop." Correspondents spend a lot of their time trying to place loans with a group of insurance companies. The insurance company is in the insurance business. The insurance company does not want to be in the commercial real estate origination business. They will provide the money to make loans, but they don't want to service those loans, nor do they want to go through the solicitation process that we go through. They sell insurance, they collect premiums, and that bucket of money they have needs to be invested. One of the ways is by making mortgages through correspondents.

Correspondent shops essentially have a license, allowing the correspondent to be one of only a few companies in a region that can accept, analyze and submit deals to the insurance company they're tied to. Usually, a correspondent shop might have 8, 9, or even 10 different insurance companies that have a little bit of a variation on the theme of the products and/or loans they offer.

When you call one of those insurance companies directly, they'll route you back to that correspondent shop. This is fine because, in many cases, the correspondent shop will do a lot of the work. The big difference is, of course, they need to earn a fee. You'll be sharing a fee with them, which could be good or bad; but basically you're giving your client away because, after they make the loan, they service the loan. The insurance company doesn't want to be in the servicing business either, so the correspondent shop might have a 100 million or 200 million or a billion-dollar portfolio of loans they have made and are servicing. They make a little bit of a strip of income from that servicing portfolio, and of course, they're collecting the mortgage, and they have a built-in relationship with a Borrower.

Sounds great. However, insurance companies are generally conservative Lenders, maybe 60–70% loan to value. The rates may or may not be competitive with banks, so they may not be the best alternative or money source. The correspondent shops do have a nice cozy relationship of built-in business because of their servicing portfolio and the direct relations with the provider of the funds. On the other hand, at times, they're not that competitive.

In my experience, when I've interviewed and hired people from correspondent shops, what has happened is a correspondent shop will hire someone, and the pitch is, "Hey, we own the shop. We've been doing this for a very long time, and boy, we're doing all this insurance company business, and we have all this other business that we're turning away. You come to join us, and you can have that other business that we've turned away." On the surface, it's a compelling argument. But what I've seen, when I interview people who are not so happy in a correspondent shop, is that the "other business" that's being turned away doesn't fit the insurance company's credit box. But keep in mind the entire business support systems and resources are aimed at keeping the insurance company deal flow. So, the originator begins to feel isolated and out of the loop—in part, because all the other people in the company aren't in the market other than the insurance company market, so they can't help with non-insurance company market information or Lender contacts.

Embedded Shops

At CBRE and Marcus and Millichap, there are companies within companies. The way MMCC started was they were going to have one or two mortgage originators in an office, and those originators were going to get leads and get business from the sales agents in the office.

It sounds good, and it worked to some degree. If someone is competent in that office, they're doing very, very well at getting a lot of business following a trial period of trustworthiness. In other words, sales agents are not eager to refer business to someone who has not earned their trust. Proving competency and proving trust are the number-one priority.

A lot of the brokers are incredibly competitive, and they're not going to just simply give an originator their lists of clients. It's just not going to happen. Also, many sales agents see no upside in recommending an in-house mortgage broker, for fear if something goes wrong, the client will blame them. Some sales agents do not see any upside. You must prove yourself first. If you can prove yourself, over time, it could be a very lucrative situation.

I can't speak to CBRE because I had never been in that shop. They have a little bit of an advantage in that they have an agency license. In other words, they are seller-servicers and Delegated Underwriters for Freddie and Fannie. This means they are making credit decisions internally at their shops, which Marcus doesn't do. Marcus acts as a broker by trying to place loans with the best Lender at any given point in time. Whereas CBRE, if it's multifamily, can make credit decisions. A little bit of a difference, but again, you get the point.

Independent Lenders

Sort of an outlier, and something you need to look out for, is those Lenders that purport to lend directly. These are generally not banks. They might be specialty Lenders, opportunistic Lenders; and sometimes you must ask: Are they purely Lenders, or are they brokers too? You must be very, very careful. In the Northeast, what I had found when I came back from California was that Lenders, if they could not do a deal, would share that information with another Lender friend of theirs, unless you explicitly stated that they do not share. It's called a "Lender turn down." In effect, it is a deal that they are turning away, but they will show it to a friend at another bank. I have found that the Lender turndown lead generation model is alive and well in some areas of the country. Be careful not to lose control, and know your banker.

That's an overview of the different models you'll see out there. Each has a positive and each has a negative. I encourage you to do your homework and due diligence on your competition.

COMPETITORS	PROFILE DEFINES INEFFICIENCY
Lenders	Regulated and specialty Lenders employ loan officers protecting a credit box. Limited flexibility.
Correspondents	Dedicated to originating and serving loans for a handful of insurance companies.
Embedded	Unable to effectively solicity from other brokerage brands, limiting success to successful office location.
Independents	Unable or unwilling to scale.

NOTES

EXPAND YOUR KNOWLEDGE

E-Learning Series

Learn more about our E-Learning Series at
Silverthread Capital University:

www.SilverthreadCapitalU.com

Personal Coaching

For more information on one-on-one, high impact coaching,
please e-mail the author, Adam Petriella, at:

apetriella@silverthreadcapital.com

Team Training

If you are an agency owner, broker, or sales manager
and would like more information on team training,
please e-mail the author, Adam Petriella, at:

apetriella@silverthreadcapital.com

APPENDICES

RESOURCES

The following appendices are example forms, letters, and tools designed to help you succeed. You can find these resources as stand-alone files on the Silverthread Capital University website.

Access valuable downloads at
www.SilverthreadCapitalU.com

Look for the word **"Appendix"** at the bottom of the Website. Click. Create log in account and get exclusive access to valuable files.

Appendix 1.1.
Exclusive Fee Agreement (Example)

DATE: July 15, 2014

RE: Engagement of **Silverthread Capital Corporation** ("Silverthread") as the exclusive representative ("Intermediary") for <<Insert Details>> as a prospective Borrower ("Borrower") for the purpose of arranging financing, relating to the real property located at <<Insert Details>> known commonly as subject ("Property").

Dear <<Insert Name>>:

Thank you for allowing Silverthread to arrange financing on the above-referenced Property. We look forward to working with you on this transaction and will proceed with the following terms:

Financing Terms

Borrower is seeking financing in the approximate aggregate amount of $<<Insert Details>>.

Exclusivity Period

Borrower grants Silverthread the exclusive right to arrange financing and to contact prospective financing sources on Borrower's behalf. The exclusive relationship will last for a period of <<Insert Details>> days from execution of this agreement (the "Exclusivity Period"). Should any prospective Lender or another real estate financing Intermediary contact Borrower during the Exclusivity Period, Borrower will refer said Lender/Intermediary to Silverthread. If, at the expiration of the Exclusivity Period, a prospective Lender has not been selected and an application/commitment is not being pursued, Silverthread will furnish to Owner a list of prospective Lenders to whom Silverthread has submitted the Property for financing. Said list will be provided within 10 business days. If within twelve (12) months following such expiration, a funding is consummated by Borrower with a Lender (or an affiliate of Lender) named in said list, Silverthread will be deemed to have earned a fee payable in the amount and manner outlined in this agreement.

Fee and Reimbursable Third-Party Out-of-Pocket Expenses

Fee is one hundred basis points (1.00%) of the final negotiated loan amount. Silverthread fee is earned upon Borrower's acceptance of a commitment issued by a Lender, however conditioned, and, therefore, if the loan does not close solely due to a default by Borrower under the terms of any written commitment entered into with the Lender, Silverthread fee will be immediately due and payable. Except as noted in the preceding sentence, Silverthread fee is payable upon the closing of the loan or, in the case of multiple loan fundings, upon the initial funding of the first draw, and the Borrower hereby authorizes the title company, escrow agent, or other closing agent to pay the fee to Silverthread at closing.

Should Borrower apply for financing with another broker during the term of this agreement and eventually fund a loan without Silverthread as Intermediary, Silverthread will be due a breakage fee of 50% of the agreed-upon fee. Upon the closing of a mortgage on the Property, Silverthread is authorized (at its own expense) to issue news releases and to publish announcements in newspapers, trade journals, and other media.

Arbitration of Disputes

If a controversy arises with respect to the subject matter of this Financing Agreement (including but not limited to the disbursement of the deposit or payment of the fee as provided herein), Borrower and Silverthread agree that such controversy shall be settled by final, binding arbitration in accordance with the Commercial Arbitration Rules of the American Arbitration Association, and judgment upon the award rendered by the arbitrator(s) may be entered in any court having jurisdiction thereof.

In the event Silverthread is successful in obtaining financing for the Property, then Borrower agrees that Silverthread shall be granted an exclusive right to negotiate, for Borrower

or any of its affiliates, any future financing commitment from the institution that issues the commitment, for one year from the date of the closing of the loan.

Both parties agree to keep the contents of this agreement confidential, provided that Silverthread may disclose the contents of the agreement in connection with the payment or collection of its fee and either party may disclose information to prospective Lenders and their respective attorneys, accountants, or other financial advisors in connection with performing their obligations hereunder.

Please sign and date this agreement and retain a copy for your files. This agreement may be signed in counterparts, and facsimile signatures may be deemed as original signatures. If you have any questions regarding this agreement, please do not hesitate to call.

Sincerely,

_____

SILVERTHREAD

Agreed and accepted as of the <<Insert >> day of <<Insert Month>>, <<Insert Year>>.

NAME: << Insert Details>>

TITLE: Borrower

DATE: << Insert Details>>

BY: << Insert Details>>

     Its authorized representative

Appendix 1.2
Non-Exclusive Fee Agreement (Example)

We have included our "non-exclusive" agreement. We generally use these agreements with less sophisticated, non-institutional investors. The tone of the letter is more approachable and sounds less like a legal document than a general businessperson's common sense agreement stating what services you will provide and the expected obligation and compensation paid by Borrower.

June 5, 2019

Borrower Name:

Dear CLIENT:

Thank you for working with Silverthread Capital Corporation to source financing for XYZ.

To locate the best available borrowing terms for you, we are preparing a memo to Lenders which will include information provided by you to Silverthread. We respect your privacy and will release the information solely to credible lending sources we interview by phone or in person. We will provide you with periodic updates and occasionally have additional questions for you from Lenders.

Currently, we know Lenders are providing loans for properties like yours, but because the market is dynamic and Lender "appetites" change, we will research, locate, interview, and assess additional lending sources to choose from. Should any Lenders contact you based on Silverthread efforts, you agree to refer them back to Silverthread to discuss their lending terms.

Our goal is to provide you with a "Lender matrix" containing a minimum of three quotes, if available, from credible sources.

If you decide to move forward with any Lender sourced by Silverthread, we will coordinate the document collection and ongoing processing of the loan and will problem-solve and negotiate any potential issues that may arise with the Lender or any third-party providers such as appraisers, engineers, inspectors, and the like. We are working on your behalf to accomplish your goals.

Silverthread Capital Corporation earns a professional services fee of 1% of the loan amount, paid by the Borrower at funding, for any Lender sourced by Silverthread. If you decide to pursue Lenders on your own, please notify us right away. If you locate funding based upon work product provided to you by Silverthread, such as financing memo or "Lender matrix," a fee of 0.5% shall be due to Silverthread Capital Corporation.

Thank you, and again, we look forward to continuing to work together with you to accomplish your goals.

Agreed:

Name: _____

Authorized Borrower Signature: _____

Date: _____

Silverthread Capital Corp. _____

Date: _____

Appendix 2.1. Financing Memo (Example)

REQUEST FOR FI-NANCING: $1,112,000

PURPOSE: Cash Out Refi

PROPERTY ADDRESS: 540 XYZ Ave

PROPERTY DESCRIPTION: The subject property is an approximate 7,000sf multi-tenant office building recently fully renovated immediately after owner took possession last year.

SPONSOR: Sponsor reported credit of 806.

Biography of Owner

CURRENT SENIOR DEBT:	$0
NEW FINANCING AMOUNT REQUESTED:	$1,112,000
LTV REQUESTED:	75%
DSCR:	1.3
INTEREST:	4.5%
TERM:	5-yr
AMORTIZATION:	25-yr
SCHEDULED GROSS INCOME 2019:	$153,420
NET INCOME:	$96,480

Appendix 2.2. Financing Memo Middle Form Light Analysis (Example)

CONFIDENTIAL RE-QUEST FOR FINANCING

PROJECT NAME

555 Elm St., Glendale, CA 91204

A XX-UNIT APARTMENT PROJECT

PRESENTED BY:

NAME

OFFICE STREET ADDRESS

SUITE XXX

CITY, STATE, ZIP

PHONE NO.

<name>@_____.com

Confidentiality and Disclaimer

The information contained in the following memorandum is proprietary and strictly confidential. It is intended to be reviewed only by the party receiving it from Silverthread Capital and should not be made available to any other person or entity without the written consent of Silverthread Capital. This memorandum has been prepared to provide summary, unverified information to prospective Lenders, and to establish only a preliminary level of interest in the subject property. The information contained herein is not a substitute for a thorough due diligence investigation. Silverthread Capital has not made any investigation, and makes no warranty or representation, with respect to the income or expenses for the subject property, the future projected financial performance of the property, the size and square footage of the property and improvements, the presence or absence of contaminating substances, PCBs or asbestos, the compliance with State and Federal regulations, the physical condition of the improvements thereon, or the financial condition or business prospects of any tenant, or any tenant's plans or intentions to continue its occupancy of the subject property. The information contained in this memorandum has been obtained from sources we believe to be reliable; however, Silverthread Capital has not verified, and will not verify, any of the information contained herein, nor has Silverthread Capital conducted any investigation regarding these matters and makes no warranty or representation whatsoever regarding the accuracy or completeness of the information provided. All potential Lenders must take appropriate measures to verify all of the information set forth herein.

Table of Contents

NOTE: Include page numbers to make navigation easier.

Executive Summary

XYZ LLC has retained Silverthread Capital Corporation to arrange for the recapitalization of a 51-unit multi-family property located in Houston, TX. We are seeking a fixed rate term loan with a 30-year amortization at best market rate.

Project Name	Insert details
Project Address	Insert details
Purpose of Loan	Insert details
Loan Amount Requested	Insert details
Term Requested	Insert details
Amortization Requested	Insert details
Interest Rate Requested	Insert details
Current Market Value of Asset	Insert details
LTV	Insert details
DSCR	Insert details
Debt Yield	Insert details
Gross Square Feet	Insert details
Loan Per Foot	Insert details
Property Condition (Fair, Good, Excellent)	Insert details

Borrower/Sponsor

XYZ LLC, a Texas Limited Liability Company and its Managing Member over the past 15 years, has successfully purchased, rehabbed and sold for profit several multifamily assets in Houston, Texas. The managing member is the sole owner and manager of the subject property. In addition to the subject property, the Borrower owns an SFR in which he resides.

Borrower Motivation

The Borrower traded into the subject property using a 1031 Tax Deferred Exchange. He closed escrow in January of 2019 using hard money to take advantage of a buying opportunity that was the Northline 51-unit subject property. He needed to move quickly. The Borrower would like to pay off the existing senior loan with a conventional term loan.

Building and Site

The subject property is a two-story, xx-unit apartment building that is currently xx% occupied. The overall design and tenant appeal are typical of the neighborhood. Ingress/egress is via a curb-cut driveway on <street name>. The property has been adequately maintained, and no deferred repairs were observed.

Location

The subject property is situated in the City of < >, < > County, and lies approximately xx miles east of downtown <city name—if a major MSA that affects the property>. The surrounding area is approximately 90% built out, with single-family residences accounting for approximately 75% of the land use.

Located two miles west of the on/off ramps to Interstate Route 66, the subject site is a mid-block <corner> parcel situated on the northern side <NWC> of <street name>, approximately 100 feet north of Main Street. The site is bounded on the south by <street name>, on the north by an adjacent retail strip center, and on the west and east by adjacent apartment buildings of comparable size and quality.

Management of the Property

The Borrower has a 15-year history of multifamily property management and will self-manage the property.

Transaction Strengths

- Borrower with a successful track record of multifamily ownership.
- Minimal deferred maintenance.
- Income upside.
- Homogeneous neighborhood.

Transaction Weaknesses

- Sponsor liquidity.

Mitigating Factors

- Stable cash flow
- Nearly 100% Occupancy

Photos

TOP VIEW

**STREET SCENE
LOOKING NORTH**

(SUBJECT ON RIGHT)

**STREET SCENE
LOOKING SOUTH**

(SUBJECT ON LEFT)

Maps

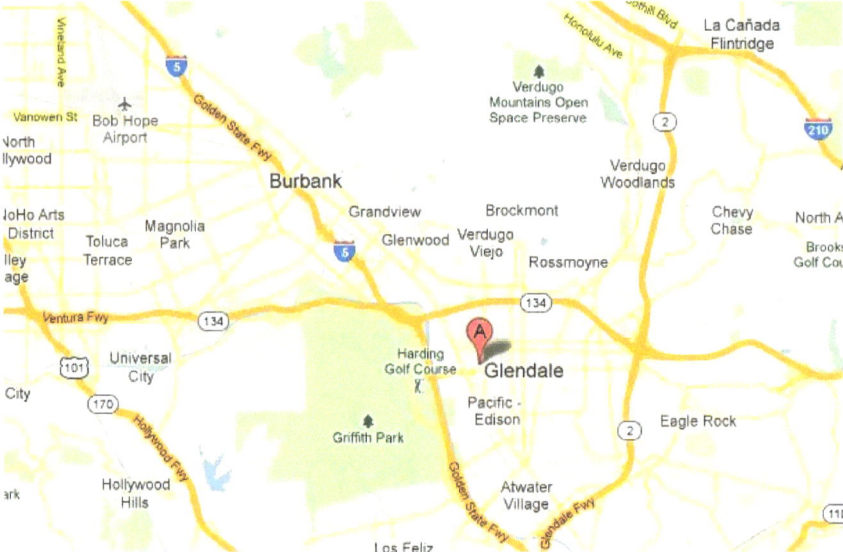

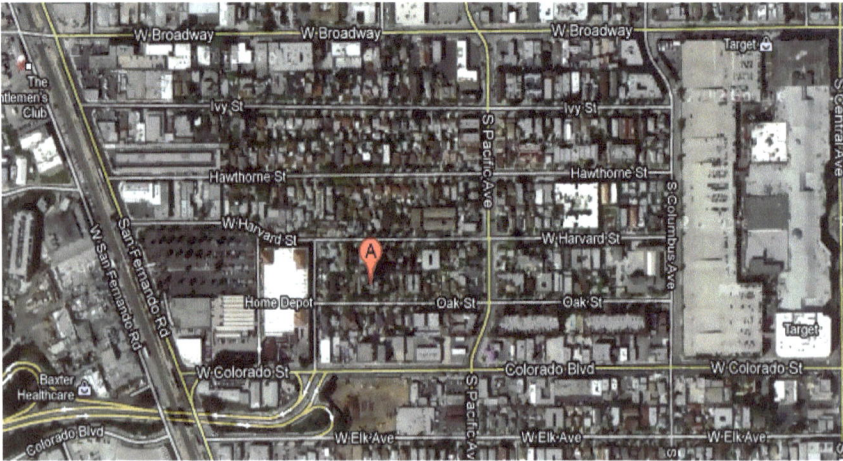

Appendix 3. Term Sheet (Example)

PRELIMINARY SINGLE-TENANT LOAN QUOTE

Date of Quote:	4/20/2017
Borrowing Entity:	A yet-to-be determined entity acceptable by Lender
Lender:	Name of Lender Here
Loan Purpose:	Cash-out refinance
Property Location:	45 Park Place
Tenant:	Name of Tenant Here
Lease Guarantor:	Corporate Lease
Building Size:	19,235 square feet
Lot Size:	2.18 acres
Total Loan Amount:	$2,275,000
Lease Commencement Date:	6/12/2003
Original Lease Term:	15 years
Current Lease Expiry:	1/31/2025
Extension Options Remaining:	Four (4) extensions at five (5) years each. Each extension will add $1.00 to annual gross rent payments.
Lease Term Remaining:	91 months (from 6/1/2017)
Est. Loan Balance @ Loan Maturity (Est. Date: 5/1/27)	$1,470,568
Est. Loan Balance @ Lease Expiry (Est. Date: 1/31/25)	$1,693,773
Initial Annual Gross Rental Income:	$276,000
Lease Type:	NNN
Estimated Market Value:	$3,900,000

Maximum LTV:	Maximum 65% of "As-Is" leased fee value; no greater than 75% of Dark Value to be determined by appraiser
Minimum DSC:	1.35x
Loan Term:	10 years (120 months)
Cash Sweep:	Net cash flow from property to go into a Lender-controlled account beginning 12 months prior to lease rollover (1/31/2024), unless next lease extension is executed prior to this date
Rate Index:	10 Year LIBOR Swap Rate
Spread:	320 bps; interest rate floor of 5.50%
Indicative Rate:	5.50%
Lender Fees:	None
Prepayment Penalty:	9.5 Year / yield maintenance
Amortization Period:	240 months (20 years)
Costs:	Standard third party costs
Recourse:	Non-recourse
Primary Collateral:	1st Mortgage/assignment of rents
Reporting Requirements:	N/A
Underwriting:	Subject to satisfactory review of lease, Lender comfort with tenant, and final approval of tenant and guarantor financial capacity

Appendix 4. Lender Matrix Quotes (Example)

Rate Type Debt Quotes

PROPERTY TYPE	SUBJECT PROPERTY STREET ADDRESS, CITY, STATE ZIP
Insert details	Insert details

PROPERTY IMAGE HERE	*PROPERTY IMAGE HERE*	*PROPERTY IMAGE HERE*

DEBT OPTIONS	OPTION 1	OPTION 2	OPTION 3	OPTION 4
Loan Amount:	Insert details	Insert details	Insert details	Insert details
Loan Term:	Insert details	Insert details	Insert details	Insert details
Fixed Term:	Insert details	Insert details	Insert details	Insert details
Floating Term:	Insert details	Insert details	Insert details	Insert details
Interest Rate:	Insert details	Insert details	Insert details	Insert details
Rate Type:	Insert details	Insert details	Insert details	Insert details
Estimated Value:	Insert details	Insert details	Insert details	Insert details
LTV:	Insert details	Insert details	Insert details	Insert details
Amortization:	Insert details	Insert details	Insert details	Insert details
Maturity:	Insert details	Insert details	Insert details	Insert details
Monthly Payment:	Insert details	Insert details	Insert details	Insert details
Annual Payment:	Insert details	Insert details	Insert details	Insert details
Recourse:	Insert details	Insert details	Insert details	Insert details
Minimum DSCR:	Insert details	Insert details	Insert details	Insert details
PPP:	Insert details	Insert details	Insert details	Insert details
Estimated Closing Costs:	Insert details	Insert details	Insert details	Insert details
Lender Fee:	Insert details	Insert details	Insert details	Insert details
Comments:	Insert details			
Contact:	Insert details			

Appendix 5. Commercial Loan Application

RESOURCES

Due to the complex nature of this document, we've only included a few images as an example. You are encouraged to download and review this Commercial Loan Application example and other documents from the Silverthread Capital University website.

Access valuable downloads at
www.SilverthreadCapitalU.com

Look for the word **"Appendix"** at the bottom of the Website. Click. Create log-in account and get exclusive access to valuable files.

Commercial Loan Application

I.	PERSONAL OR BORROWING ENTITY INFORMATION

Complete this section for all guarantors and spouse or non-spouse, if applicable. (Attach additional sheets if needed.)
Additional guarantors must complete sections I, V - XI

Borrower is an:	☐ Individual(s)	☐ Entity			
Borrowing entity is a:	☐ Corporation (C Corp)	☐ LLC	☐ LP/LLP	☐ S Corp	☐ Other:
Borrowing Entity Name:		Date Formed:		Tax ID:	

Any individual who owns 25% or more of the borrowing entity is required to be a guarantor of the loan.
Please list ALL additional owners below or attach organization chart.

Name	Ownership	On Title	Is the structure of the entity changing as part of the loan transaction? ☐ Yes ☐ No
	%	☐ Yes ☐ No	If yes, please describe:
	%	☐ Yes ☐ No	
	%	☐ Yes ☐ No	
	%	☐ Yes ☐ No	

Borrower Name:			Co-Borrower Name:		
Social Security #:	Date of Birth:		Social Security #:	Date of Birth:	
Marital Status: ☐ Married ☐ Single ☐ Divorced			Marital Status: ☐ Married ☐ Single ☐ Divorced		
Address 1:			Address 1:		
Address 2:			Address 2:		
City: State: Zip:			City: State: Zip:		
Phone Number:			Phone Number:		
Email Address:			Email Address:		

II.	LOAN REQUEST

Commercial Mortgage Type Applied For:	☐ Investor	☐ Owner-Occupied

Loan Purpose: ☐ Purchase ☐ Refinance ☐ Cash-out Refinance	Amortization: ☐ 15 Years ☐ 20 Years ☐ 25 Years ☐ 30 Years

Requested Loan Amount: _____   Requested Interest Rate %: _____

Loan Program ☐ 5 Year   ☐ 7 Year   **Prepayment Type:** ☐ 5% for 3 Years   ☐ 5% for 5 Years ☐ Declining 5%, 4%, 3%, 2%, 1%

If a Purchase:	If a Refinance:	Subject Property Cash Flow:
Purchase Contract Expires:	Original Purchase Date:	Actual Rents in Place (annualized): $
Purchase Price: $	Original Purchase Price: $	Less Actual Expenses (annualized): $
Amount of Down Payment: $	Cost of Improvements Made*: $	Equals Net Op. Income (annualized): $ 0
	Current Lender:	Gross Annual Rent of Largest Tenant: $
	Interest Rate %:	Annual Property & Liability Insurance Premium: $
	Monthly Payment: $	Annual Property Taxes: $
	Pay-Off Mortgage 1: $	*Please do not include mortgage payment or depreciation as a part of the Actual Expenses above.
	Pay-Off Mortgage 2: $	
	Pay-Off Outstanding Taxes/Others: $	
	Cash Out: $	
	Cash Out Description:	
	Is the property subject to any additional liens, encumbrances or restrictions? ☐ Yes ☐ No	
	If yes, please explain:	

III. SUBJECT PROPERTY INFORMATION

Subject Property Address:

City:	State:	Zip:		Year Built:

Description of Subject Property (attach description if necessary):

Commercial Property Type:

☐ Multifamily	☐ Mixed Use (>50% Residential)	☐ Warehouse	☐ Retail	☐ Restaurants
☐ Mobile Home Parks	☐ Mixed Use (<50% Residential)	☐ Light Industrial	☐ Office	☐ Bars
☐ Automotive	☐ Self Storage	☐ Daycare Center	☐ Other	

1-4 Investment Property Type:

☐ Single Family Residence	☐ Residential Condo	☐ Townhouse	☐ Multifamily 2-4 Unit	☐ PUD

Does the property have? ☐ Underground or above ground storage tanks ☐ Automotive repair uses ☐ Ongoing environmental remediation

☐ Hazardous material handling/Licensing ☐ On-site dry cleaner ☐ A prior Phase 1 report available ☐ N/A

Estimated Value of Real Estate: $	
Source of Value Estimate: ☐ Appraisal ☐ Estimate ☐ Sales Price (if purchase)	
Owner Occupied: ☐ Yes ☐ No	Owner Occupancy %:
Yrs. of Investor Experience:	Number of Buildings:
Number of Units:	Building Sq. Footage:
Number of Units Occupied:	Land Sq. Footage:

IV. BUSINESS INFORMATION

Please complete if you are Self-Employed or the Borrower is a Business Entity.

Business Name:

Address:

City:	State:	Zip:

Years as Business Owner:

Will this business occupy the subject property? ☐ Yes ☐ No

Type of Business: ☐ Corporation (C Corp) ☐ LLC ☐ LP/LLP ☐ S Corp ☐ Other

Tax Year 1 20____ Business Income		Tax Year 2 20____ Business Income	
a. Annual Revenues:	$	a. Annual Revenues:	$
b. Annual Expenses: (Exclude depreciation)	$	b. Annual Expenses: (Exclude depreciation)	$
Net Operating Income (A-B)	$ 0	Net Operating Income (A-B)	$ 0

V. EMPLOYMENT INFORMATION

Self Employed: ☐ Yes ☐ No	Self Employed: ☐ Yes ☐ No
Years on the Job:	Years on the Job:

VI. ANNUAL INCOME AND COMBINED HOUSING EXPENSE INFORMATION

Net ANNUAL Income:	Borrower	Co-Borrower	Combined MONTHLY Housing Expenses (for Primary Residence only)	
Total Income:	$	$	Total Monthly Housing:	$

VII. ASSETS AND LIABILITIES

Assets		Liabilities	
Total Assets:	$	Total Liabilities:	$
Total Cash Available: (Savings and Checking)	$	Net Worth:	$ 0

VIII. PERSONAL DECLARATIONS

If you answer "Yes" to any questions A through F, please provide a separate explanation.	Borrower		Co-Borrower	
A. Are there any outstanding judgments against you?	☐ Yes	☐ No	☐ Yes	☐ No
B. Have you declared bankruptcy within the last 4 years?	☐ Yes	☐ No	☐ Yes	☐ No
C. Have you had property foreclosed upon or given title in lieu thereof in the last 4 years?	☐ Yes	☐ No	☐ Yes	☐ No
D. Are you party to a lawsuit?	☐ Yes	☐ No	☐ Yes	☐ No
E. Have you directly or indirectly been obligated on any loan which resulted in foreclosure, transfer of title in lieu of foreclosure or judgment in the last 4 years?	☐ Yes	☐ No	☐ Yes	☐ No
F. Are you presently delinquent or in default on any Federal debt or any other loan, mortgage, financial obligation or loan guarantee?	☐ Yes	☐ No	☐ Yes	☐ No
G. Are you obligated to pay alimony, child support or separate maintenance?	☐ Yes	☐ No	☐ Yes	☐ No
H. If applicable, do you intend to occupy the property as your primary housing residence?	☐ Yes	☐ No	☐ Yes	☐ No
I. Have you been convicted of a felony within the past 10 years?	☐ Yes	☐ No	☐ Yes	☐ No
J. Are you a U.S. citizen?	☐ Yes	☐ No	☐ Yes	☐ No
K. Are you a permanent resident alien?	☐ Yes	☐ No	☐ Yes	☐ No

If you answered no to questions J and K, please provide visa status:

IX. BUSINESS DECLARATIONS
Please select N/A if you are closing as an individual and your business is not going to occupy the subject property.

Neither my business, nor any principal of my business has declared bankruptcy in the last 4 years.	☐ True	☐ False	☐ N/A
Neither my business, nor any principle of my business is a party to any lawsuit.	☐ True	☐ False	☐ N/A
My business has never defaulted on any Federal debt including SBA loans.	☐ True	☐ False	☐ N/A
No principle of my business has had a property foreclosed within the past 4 years.	☐ True	☐ False	☐ N/A
The business has neither been denied a license, certification or ability to conduct business nor been suspended or administratively limited to its ability to conduct business.	☐ True	☐ False	☐ N/A

Please explain any declaration with "false" response
or provide documentation:

X. GENERAL AUTHORIZATION

I HEREBY AUTHORIZE LENDER TO VERIFY ANY AND ALL INFORMATION PROVIDED OR REQUESTED WITH THIS APPLICATION, INCLUDING BUT NOT LIMITED TO MY PAST AND PRESENT EMPLOYMENT, EARNING RECORDS, BANK ACCOUNTS, STOCK HOLDINGS AND ANY OTHER ASSET BALANCES NEEDED TO PROCESS MY LOAN APPLICATION.

I UNDERSTAND THAT FALSE INFORMATION AND STATEMENTS MAY RESULT IN POSSIBLE PROSECUTION UNDER FEDERAL AND STATE LAWS. FURTHER, I UNDERSTAND THAT MY INFORMATION WILL BE SCRUBBED AGAINST THE OFAC, SDN LISTS, EXCLUSIONARY AND OTHER LISTS TO CONFIRM COMPLIANCE WITH THE US PATRIOT ACT, COUNTER-TERRORISM REGULATIONS AND BSA/AML REGULATIONS.

I CERTIFY BY SIGNING BELOW THAT THIS IS NOT AN APPROVAL OR COMMITMENT TO LEND AND THAT I MAY BE DENIED AT ANY TIME DURING THE PROCESS FOR REASONS INCLUDING BUT NOT LIMITED TO CREDIT WORTHINESS SUCH AS: COLLATERAL ISSUES, BUSINESS PRACTICES OR UNSTABLE GOVERNMENT/POLITICAL CLIMATE WITHIN A COUNTRY.

Applicant
I AUTHORIZE LENDER TO MAKE ALL INQUIRES NECESSARY THAT VERIFY THE ACCURACY OF THE STATEMENTS MADE HEREIN AND TO DETERMINE MY CREDITWORTHINESS.

Applicant Authorization/Signature: _____ Social Sec. #: _____ Date: _____

Co-Applicant
I AUTHORIZE LENDER TO MAKE ALL INQUIRES NECESSARY THAT VERIFY THE ACCURACY OF THE STATEMENTS MADE HEREIN AND TO DETERMINE MY CREDITWORTHINESS.

Co-Applicant Authorization/Signature _____ Social Sec. # _____ Date: _____

X. INFORMATION FOR GOVERNMENT MONITORING PURPOSES

The purpose of collecting this information is to help ensure that all applicants are treated fairly and that the housing needs of communities and neighborhoods are being fulfilled. For residential mortgage lending, federal law requires that we ask applicants for their demographic information (ethnicity, sex, and race) in order to monitor our compliance with equal credit opportunity, fair housing, and home mortgage disclosure laws. You are not required to provide this information, but are encouraged to do so. **The law provides that we may not discriminate** on the basis of this information, or on whether you choose to provide it. However, if you choose not to provide the information and you have made this application in person, federal regulations require us to note your ethnicity, sex, and race on the basis of visual observation or surname. The law also provides that we may not discriminate on the basis of age or marital status information you provide on this application.
Instructions: You may select one or more "Hispanic or Latino" origins and one or more designations for "Race." If you do not wish to provide some or all of this information, select the applicable check box.

BORROWER

ETHNICITY
- ☐ Hispanic or Latino
- ☐ Mexican ☐ Puerto Rican ☐ Cuban
- ☐ Other Hispanic or Latino – Enter Origin:

Examples: Argentinian, Colombian, Dominican, Nicaraguan, Salvadoran, Spaniard, etc.

- ☐ Not Hispanic or Latino
- ☐ I do not wish to provide this information

RACE
- ☐ American Indian or Alaska Native-
Enter name of enrolled or principal tribe:
- ☐ Asian
- ☐ Asian Indian ☐ Chinese ☐ Filipino
- ☐ Japanese ☐ Korean ☐ Vietnamese
Other Asian - Enter race:
Ex: Hmong, Laotian, Thai, Pakistani, Cambodian, etc.
- ☐ Black or African American
- ☐ Native Hawaiian or Other Pacific Islander
- ☐ Native Hawaiian ☐ Guamanian or Chamorro
- ☐ Samoan ☐ Other Pacific Islander -

SEX:
- ☐ Male
- ☐ Female
- ☐ I do not wish to provide this information

_Enter race _____
- ☐ White
- ☐ I do not wish to provide this information

CO-BORROWER

ETHNICITY
- ☐ Hispanic or Latino
- ☐ Mexican ☐ Puerto Rican ☐ Cuban
- ☐ Other Hispanic or Latino – Enter Origin:

Examples: Argentinian, Colombian, Dominican, Nicaraguan, Salvadoran, Spaniard, etc.

- ☐ Not Hispanic or Latino
- ☐ I do not wish to provide this information

RACE
- ☐ American Indian or Alaska Native-
Enter name of enrolled or principal tribe:
- ☐ Asian
- ☐ Asian Indian ☐ Chinese ☐ Filipino
- ☐ Japanese ☐ Korean ☐ Vietnamese
_Other Asian - Enter race _____
Ex: Hmong, Laotian, Thai, Pakistani, Cambodian, etc.
- ☐ Black or African American
- ☐ Native Hawaiian or Other Pacific Islander
- ☐ Native Hawaiian ☐ Guamanian or Chamorro
- ☐ Samoan ☐ Other Pacific Islander -

SEX:
- ☐ Male
- ☐ Female
- ☐ I do not wish to provide this information

_Enter race _____
- ☐ White
- ☐ I do not wish to provide this information

To Be Completed by Financial Institution (for application taken in person):

Was the ethnicity of the Borrower collected on the basis of visual observation or surname? ☐ NO ☐ YES
Was the sex of the Borrower collected on the basis of visual observation or surname? ☐ NO ☐ YES
Was the race of the Borrower collected on the basis of visual observation or surname? ☐ NO ☐ YES

The Demographic Information was provided through:

- ☐ Face-to-Face Interview (includes Electronic Media w/Video Component)
- ☐ Telephone Interview
- ☐ Fax or Mail
- ☐ Email

Closing Notes: (1) IRS Form 4506T to be signed prior to underwriting for all borrowers and businesses related to the transaction. (2) Signatures on all tax returns may be completed at closing. This application is for a business purpose loan secured by commercial real estate. The undersigned specifically acknowledge and agree that (1) the loan requested by this application will be secured by a first mortgage or deed of trust on the property described herein; (2) the property will not be used for any illegal or prohibited purposes or use; (3) all statements made in this application are made for the purpose of obtaining the loan indicated herein; (4) occupation of the property will be as indicated above; (5) verification or reverification of any information contained in the application may be made at any time by the Lender, its agents, successors and assigns, either directly or through a credit reporting agency, from any source named in this application, and the original copy of this application will be retained by Lender, even if the loan is not approved; (6) the Lender, its agents, successors and assigns will rely on the information contained in the application and I/we have continuing obligation to amend and/or supplement the information provided in this application if any of the material facts which I/we have represented herein should change prior to closing; (7) in the event my/our payments on the loan indicated in this application become delinquent, the Lender, its agents, successors and assigns, may, in addition to all their other rights and remedies, report my/our name(s) and account information to a credit reporting agency; (8) ownership of the loan may be transferred to successors or assigns of the Lender without notice to me and/or the administration of the loan account may be transferred to an agent, successor or assign of the Lender with prior notice to me; (9) the Lender, its agents, successors and assigns make no representations or warranties, express or implied, to the Borrower(s) regarding the property, the condition of the property, or the value of the property; and (10) I/we understand and hereby agree that all principals of the company have been identified to the Lender and will sign the note personally guaranteeing repayment of the obligation. I/we the undersigned certify that the information provided in this loan application and in all loan documents submitted to Lender is true and correct as of the date set forth opposite my/our signature(s) on this application and acknowledge my/our understanding that any intentional or negligent misrepresentation of the information contained in this application may result in civil liability and/or criminal penalties including, but not limited to, fine or imprisonment or both under the provisions of Title 18, United States Code, Section 1001, et seq. and liability for monetary damages to the Lender, its agents, successors and assigns, insurers and any other person who may suffer any loss due to reliance upon any misrepresentation which I/we have made on this application.

Notice: The federal Equal Credit Opportunity Act prohibits creditors from discriminating against credit applicants on the basis of race, color, religion, national origin, sex, sexual orientation, marital status, age (provided the applicant has the capacity to enter into a binding contract); because all or part of the applicant's income derives from any public assistance program; or because the applicant has in good faith exercised any right under the Consumer Credit Protection Act. The federal agency that administers compliance with this law concerning this creditor is Federal Trade Commission, Equal Credit Opportunity, Washington, D.C., 20580.

Applicant's Initials: _____

Co-Applicant's Initials: _____

I. PERSONAL OR BORROWING ENTITY INFORMATION – continued.						

Co-Borrower 3 Name:			Co-Borrower 4 Name:		

Social Security #:		Date of Birth:	Social Security #:		Date of Birth:

Marital Status:	☐ Married ☐ Single ☐ Divorced	Marital Status:	☐ Married ☐ Single ☐ Divorced

Address 1:		Address 1:	
Address 2:		Address 2:	
City:	State: Zip:	City:	State: Zip:
Phone Number:		Phone Number:	
Email Address:		Email Address:	

V. EMPLOYMENT INFORMATION – continued.			

Self Employed:	☐ Yes ☐ No	Self Employed:	☐ Yes ☐ No
Years on the Job:		Years on the Job:	

VI. ANNUAL INCOME AND COMBINED HOUSING EXPENSE INFORMATION – continued.			

Net ANNUAL Income:	Co-Borrower 3	Co-Borrower 4	Combined MONTHLY Housing Expenses (for Primary Residence only)	
Total Income:	$	$	Total Monthly Housing:	$

VII. ASSETS AND LIABILITIES – continued.			

Assets		**Liabilities**	
Total Assets:	$	Total Liabilities:	$
Total Cash Available: (Savings and Checking)	$	Net Worth:	$ 0

VIII. PERSONAL DECLARATIONS – continued.				

If you answer "Yes" to any questions A through F, please provide a separate explanation.	Co-Borrower 3		Co-Borrower 4	
A. Are there any outstanding judgments against you?	☐ Yes	☐ No	☐ Yes	☐ No
B. Have you declared bankruptcy within the last 4 years?	☐ Yes	☐ No	☐ Yes	☐ No
C. Have you had property foreclosed upon or given title in lieu thereof in the last 4 years?	☐ Yes	☐ No	☐ Yes	☐ No
D. Are you party to a lawsuit?	☐ Yes	☐ No	☐ Yes	☐ No
E. Have you directly or indirectly been obligated on any loan which resulted in foreclosure, transfer of title in lieu of foreclosure or judgment in the last 4 years?	☐ Yes	☐ No	☐ Yes	☐ No
F. Are you presently delinquent or in default on any Federal debt or any other loan, mortgage, financial obligation or loan guarantee?	☐ Yes	☐ No	☐ Yes	☐ No
G. Are you obligated to pay alimony, child support or separate maintenance?	☐ Yes	☐ No	☐ Yes	☐ No
H. If applicable, do you intend to occupy the property as your primary housing residence?	☐ Yes	☐ No	☐ Yes	☐ No
I. Have you been convicted of a felony within the past 10 years?	☐ Yes	☐ No	☐ Yes	☐ No
J. Are you a U.S. citizen?	☐ Yes	☐ No	☐ Yes	☐ No
K. Are you a permanent resident alien?	☐ Yes	☐ No	☐ Yes	☐ No

If you answered no to questions J and K, please provide visa status.

X. GENERAL AUTHORIZATION – continued.

I HEREBY AUTHORIZE LENDER TO VERIFY ANY AND ALL INFORMATION PROVIDED OR REQUESTED WITH THIS APPLICATION, INCLUDING BUT NOT LIMITED TO MY PAST AND PRESENT EMPLOYMENT, EARNING RECORDS, BANK ACCOUNTS, STOCK HOLDINGS AND ANY OTHER ASSET BALANCES NEEDED TO PROCESS MY LOAN APPLICATION.

I UNDERSTAND THAT FALSE INFORMATION AND STATEMENTS MAY RESULT IN POSSIBLE PROSECUTION UNDER FEDERAL AND STATE LAWS FURTHER, I UNDERSTAND THAT MY INFORMATION WILL BE SCRUBBED AGAINST THE OFAC, SDN LISTS, EXCLUSIONARY AND OTHER LISTS TO CONFIRM COMPLIANCE WITH THE US PATRIOT ACT, COUNTER-TERRORISM REGULATIONS AND BSA/AML REGULATIONS

I CERTIFY BY SIGNING BELOW THAT THIS IS NOT AN APPROVAL OR COMMITMENT TO LEND AND THAT I MAY BY DENIED AT ANY TIME DURING THE PROCESS FOR REASONS INCLUDING BUT NOT LIMITED TO CREDIT WORTHINESS SUCH AS: COLLATERAL ISSUES, BUSINESS PRACTICES OR UNSTABLE GOVERNMENT/POLITICAL CLIMATE WITHIN A COUNTRY.

Applicant
I AUTHORIZE LENDER TO MAKE ALL INQUIRES NECESSARY THAT VERIFY THE ACCURACY OF THE STATEMENTS MADE   HEREIN AND TO DETERMINE MY CREDITWORTHINESS.

Applicant Authorization/Signature: _____ Social Sec. #: _____ Date: _____

Co-Applicant
I AUTHORIZE LENDER TO MAKE ALL INQUIRES NECESSARY THAT VERIFY THE ACCURACY OF THE STATEMENTS MADE   HEREIN AND TO DETERMINE MY CREDITWORTHINESS.

Co-Applicant Authorization/Signature: _____ Social Sec. #: _____ Date: _____

XI. INFORMATION FOR GOVERNMENT MONITORING PURPOSES

The purpose of collecting this information is to help ensure that all applicants are treated fairly and that the housing needs of communities and neighborhoods are being fulfilled. For residential mortgage lending, federal law requires that we ask applicants for their demographic information (ethnicity, sex, and race) in order to monitor our compliance with equal credit opportunity, fair housing, and home mortgage disclosure laws. You are not required to provide this information, but are encouraged to do so. **The law provides that we may not discriminate** on the basis of this information, or on whether you choose to provide it. However, if you choose not to provide the information and you have made this application in person, federal regulations require us to note your ethnicity, sex, and race on the basis of visual observation or surname. The law also provides that we may not discriminate on the basis or age or marital status information you provide on this application.
Instructions: You may select one or more "Hispanic or Latino" origins and one or more designations for "Race." If you do not wish to provide some or all of this information, select the applicable check box.

BORROWER

ETHNICITY
☐ Hispanic or Latino
☐ Mexican ☐ Puerto Rican ☐ Cuban
☐ Other Hispanic or Latino – Enter Origin:

_____
Examples: Argentinian, Colombian,
Dominican, Nicaraguan, Salvadoran,
Spaniard, etc

☐ Not Hispanic or Latino
☐ I do not wish to provide this information

SEX:
☐ Male
☐ Female
☐ I do not wish to provide this information

RACE
☐ American Indian or Alaska Native–
Enter name of enrolled or principal tribe.
_____
☐ Asian
☐ Asian Indian ☐ Chinese ☐ Filipino
☐ Japanese ☐ Korean ☐ Vietnamese
Other Asian - Enter race:_____
Ex: Hmong, Laotian, Thai, Pakistani, Cambodian, etc
☐ Black or African American
☐ Native Hawaiian or Other Pacific Islander
☐ Native Hawaiian ☐ Guamanian or Chamorro
☐ Samoan ☐ Other Pacific Islander –
Enter race _____
☐ White
☐ I do not wish to provide this information

CO-BORROWER

ETHNICITY
☐ Hispanic or Latino
☐ Mexican ☐ Puerto Rican ☐ Cuban
☐ Other Hispanic or Latino – Enter Origin:

_____
Examples: Argentinian, Colombian,
Dominican, Nicaraguan, Salvadoran,
Spaniard, etc

☐ Not Hispanic or Latino
☐ I do not wish to provide this information

SEX:
☐ Male
☐ Female
☐ I do not wish to provide this information

RACE
☐ American Indian or Alaska Native–
Enter name of enrolled or principal tribe.
_____
☐ Asian
☐ Asian Indian ☐ Chinese ☐ Filipino
☐ Japanese ☐ Korean ☐ Vietnamese
Other Asian - Enter race:_____
Ex: Hmong, Laotian, Thai, Pakistani, Cambodian, etc
☐ Black or African American
☐ Native Hawaiian or Other Pacific Islander
☐ Native Hawaiian ☐ Guamanian or Chamorro
☐ Samoan ☐ Other Pacific Islander –
Enter race _____
☐ White
☐ I do not wish to provide this information

To Be Completed by Financial Institution (for application taken in person):

Was the ethnicity of the Borrower collected on the basis of visual observation or surname?   ☐ NO ☐ YES
Was the sex of the Borrower collected on the basis of visual observation or surname?   ☐ NO ☐ YES
Was the race of the Borrower collected on the basis of visual observation or surname?   ☐ NO ☐ YES

The Demographic Information was provided through:

☐ Face-to-Face Interview (includes Electronic Media w/Video Component)   ☐ Fax or Mail
☐ Telephone Interview   ☐ Email

Closing Notes: (1) IRS Form 4506T to be signed prior to underwriting for all borrowers and businesses related to the transaction. (2) Signatures on all tax returns may be completed at closing. This application is for a business purpose loan secured by commercial real estate. The undersigned specifically acknowledge and agree that (1) the loan requested by this application will be secured by a first mortgage or deed of trust on the property described herein; (2) the property will not be used for any illegal or prohibited purposes or use; (3) all statements made in this application are made for the purpose of obtaining the loan indicated herein; (4) occupation of the property will be as indicated above; (5) verification or reverification of any information contained in the application may be made at any time by the Lender, its agents, successors and assigns, either directly or through a credit reporting agency, from any source named in this application, and the original copy of this application will be retained by Lender, even if the loan is not approved; (6) the Lender, its agents, successors and assigns will rely on the information contained in the application and I/we have continuing obligation to amend and/or supplement the information provided in this application if any of the material facts which I/we have represented herein should change prior to closing; (7) in the event my/our payments on the loan indicated in this application become delinquent, the Lender, its agents, successors and assigns, may, in addition to all their other rights and remedies, report my/our name(s) and account information to a credit reporting agency, (8) ownership of the loan may be transferred to successors or assigns of the Lender without notice to me and/or the administration of the loan account may be transferred to an agent, successor or assign of the Lender with prior notice to me. (9) the Lender, its agents, successors and assigns make no representations of warranties, express or implied, to the Borrower(s) regarding the property, the condition of the property, or the value of the property; and (10) I/we understand and hereby agree that all principals of the company have been identified to the Lender and will sign the note personally guaranteeing repayment of the obligation. I/we the undersigned certify that the information provided in this loan application and in all loan documents submitted to Lender is true and correct as of the date set forth opposite my/our signature(s) on this application and acknowledge my/our understanding that any intentional or negligent misrepresentation of the information contained in this application may result in civil liability and/or criminal penalties including, but not limited to, fine or imprisonment or both under the provisions of Title 18, United States Code, Section 1001, et seq, and liability for monetary damages to the Lender, its agents, successors and assigns, insurers and any other person who may suffer any loss due to reliance upon any misrepresentation which I/we have made on this application.

Notice: The federal Equal Credit Opportunity Act prohibits creditors from discriminating against credit applicants on the basis of race, color, religion, national origin, sex, sexual orientation, marital status, age (provided the applicant has the capacity to enter into a binding contract); because all or part of the applicant's income derives from any public assistance program; or because the applicant has in good faith exercised any right under the Consumer Credit Protection Act. The federal agency that administers compliance with this law concerning this creditor is Federal Trade Commission, Equal Credit Opportunity, Washington, D.C., 20580.

Co-Applicant 3 Initials: _____

Co-Applicant 4 Initials: _____

Appendix 6. A Vibrant Middle Market Opportunity

>1,531 small U.S. property acquisitions in H1 2019, representing 36.7% of all multifamily asset purchases*

> This purchase count is conservative since a notable number of transactions were under $2.5 million and therefore not included in the total.*

*CBRE

Note to Readers: This Small Balance Origination Brief is a research publication from Boxwood Means, LLC covering small balance commercial and multifamily loan transactions under $5 million. The Briefs are updated on a quarterly basis for 37 states. Boxwood deems that our data sources are reliable. Some areas of the country offer complete information than others. This report is presented on as "as is, as available" basis. Boxwood makes no warranties, expressed or implied, without limitation, to the information provided, nor are we responsible for any errors or omissions.

CY 2018: 264,000 Small Loans Funded

National Loan Volume Change, Year Over Year (%)

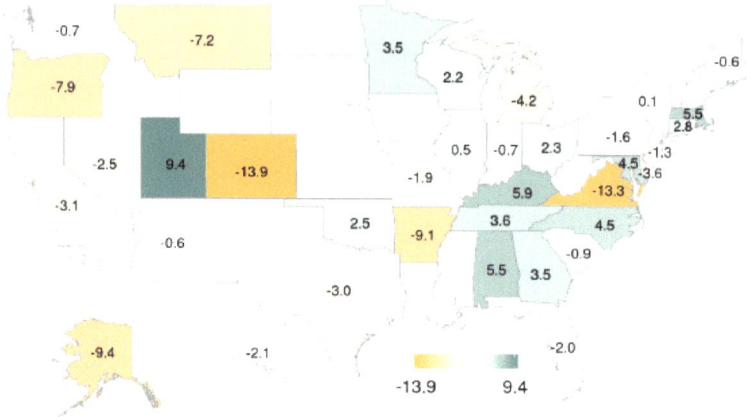

-0.7   -7.2   3.5
        2.2   -0.6
-7.9   -4.2   0.1   5.5 2.8
-2.5 9.4 -13.9   0.5 -0.7 2.3   -1.6 -1.3
-1.9   4.5 -3.6
-3.1   5.9   -13.3
2.5   3.6   4.5
-0.6 -9.1   -0.9
-3.0   5.5 3.5

-9.4   -2.1   -2.0

-13.9   9.4

Loan Type	No. Loans	Loan Volume ($B)	Volume Pct. (%)	Volume Chg. (%)	
		2018		Qtr.	YOY
Purchase	120,516	90.6	40	NA	-3.3
Refinance	143,594	134.4	60	NA	0.0
Total	**264,110**	**225.0**	**100**	**NA**	**-1.4**

Q1 2019: 47,066 Loans Funded

National Loan Volume Change, Year Over Year (%)

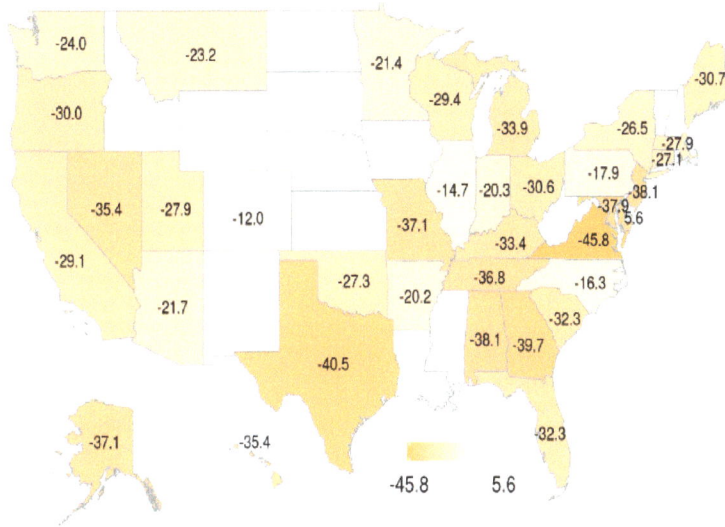

Loan Type	No. Loans	Loan Volume ($B)	Volume Pct. (%)	Volume Chg. (%)	
		Latest Quarter		Qtr.	YOY
Purchase	19,788	14.7	36	-33.1	-43.2
Refinance	27,278	26.1	64	-23.9	-17.9
Total	47,066	40.7	100	-27.5	-29.2

Q2 2019: 59,022 Loans Funded

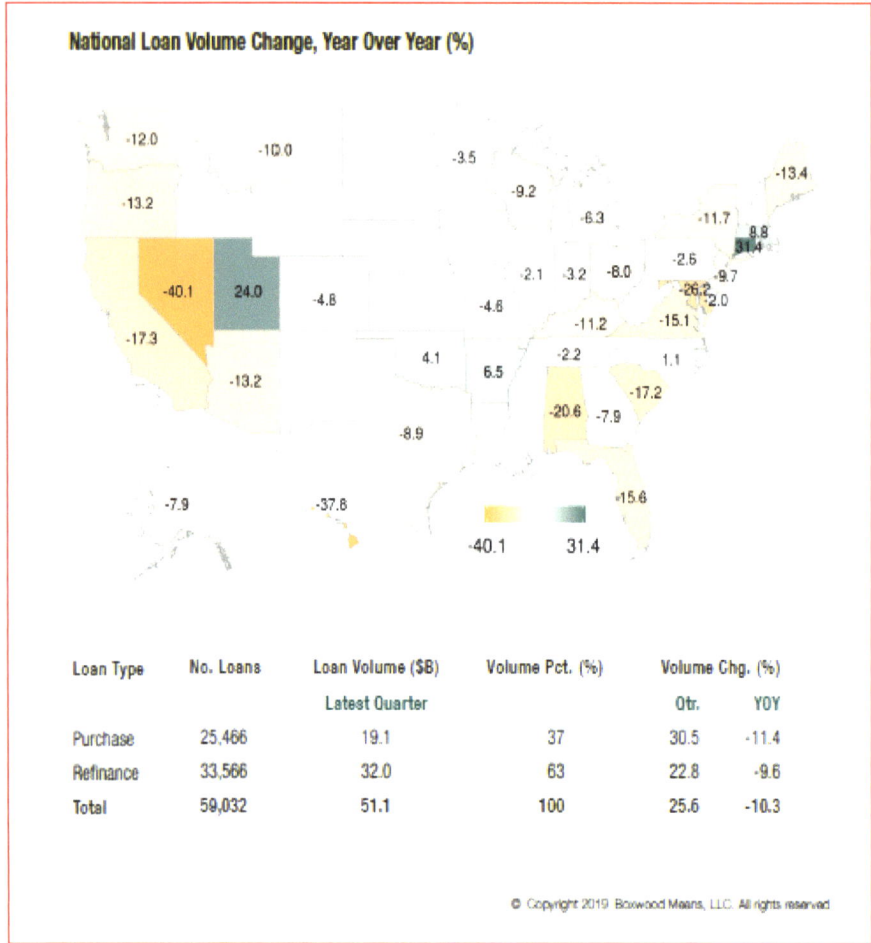

National Loan Volume Change, Year Over Year (%)

									-13.4
-12.0			-10.0		-3.5				
					-9.2		-11.7		
-13.2					-6.3			8.8 31.4	
							-2.6		
-40.1	24.0	-4.8		-2.1	-3.2	-8.0	-26.2	-9.7	
					-4.6			-2.0	
-17.3					-11.2		-15.1		
	-13.2		4.1		-2.2	1.1			
			6.5				-17.2		
		-8.9			-20.6	-7.9			

| -7.9 | -37.8 | | -15.6 |

| -40.1 | 31.4 |

Loan Type	No. Loans	Loan Volume ($B)	Volume Pct. (%)	Volume Chg. (%)	
		Latest Quarter		Qtr.	YOY
Purchase	25,466	19.1	37	30.5	-11.4
Refinance	33,566	32.0	63	22.8	-9.6
Total	59,032	51.1	100	25.6	-10.3

A FRAGMENTED MARKET SPELLS OPPORTUNITY FOR INTERMEDIARIES

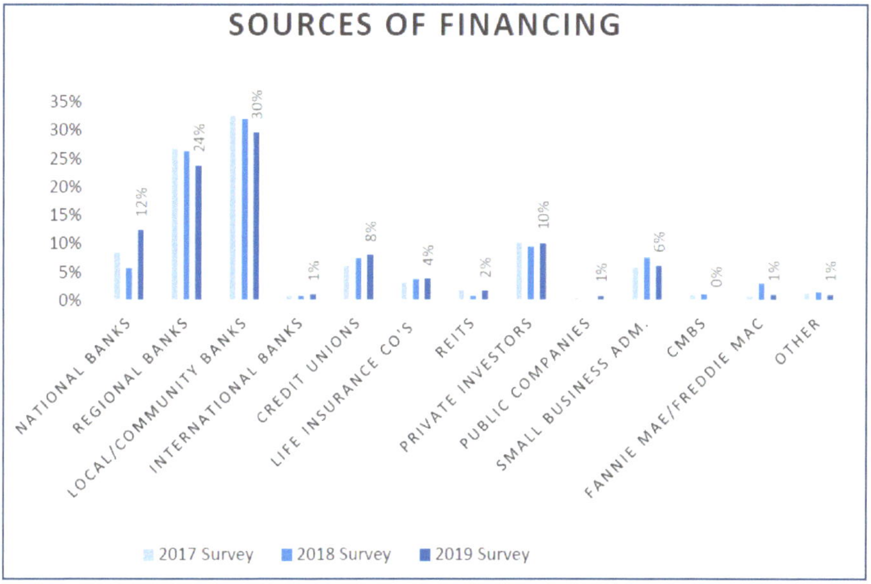
SOURCES OF FINANCING
35%
30%
25%
20%
15%
10%
5%
0%
12%
24%
30%
1%
8%
4%
2%
10%
1%
6%
0%
1%
1%
NATIONAL BANKS
REGIONAL BANKS
LOCAL/COMMUNITY BANKS
INTERNATIONAL BANKS
CREDIT UNIONS
LIFE INSURANCE CO'S
REITS
PRIVATE INVESTORS
PUBLIC COMPANIES
SMALL BUSINESS ADM.
CMBS
FANNIE MAE/FREDDIE MAC
OTHER
2017 Survey
2018 Survey
2019 Survey

Glossary

Note: *I'd like to give attribution to Mr. Blackburn for his assistance with the organization of these generally accepted and commonly used terms and concepts.*

Acceleration Clause

The section in a mortgage that says if the Borrower sells the property or places a second mortgage/mezzanine loan on the property, the bank can immediately demand to be paid in full.

Asset-Backed Security

A bond that is backed by a mixed collection of security, such as car loans, credit card paper, aircraft loans, scratch-and-dent residential loans, and subprime commercial loans.

B-Piece Buyer

The B-piece buyer is the buyer of the mortgage-backed bonds rated lower than BBB by Standard and Poor's. The B-piece is often called the first loss piece, and it is by far the riskiest investment in the offering. B-piece buyers enjoy a lot of power because, without someone to buy the first loss piece, the offering will fail. They therefore enjoy very high yields, sometimes as high as 20%. They also enjoy the right to kick weak loans out of the mortgage pool, thereby creating scratch-and-dent loans that must be sold off by the sponsor of the offering at a discount.

Bond

A bond is just a garden variety promissory note whereby a Borrower promises to pay back some money to an investor. Bonds are typically issued by companies or trusts, as opposed to by individuals.

Capital Stack

The capital stack is the sum of the first mortgage plus any second mortgage plus any mezzanine loans plus any preferred equity plus the buyer's down payment or the developer's equity contribution.

Contingency Reserve

The contingency reserve is that part of the construction loan budget that is reserved to cover cost overruns. It is usually calculated as 5% of hard and soft costs.

Credit Tenant Lease Financing (CTL Financing)

Credit tenant lease financing is a method of financing real estate at a very low interest rate. The landlord borrows money to finance the property and pledges as security the rents to be received from the investment-grade tenant. Usually the financing is structured as nonrecourse debt, and the loan is fully amortized over the term of the lease. Credit tenant leases may be created either in sale/leaseback transactions or on new purchase transactions.

Credit Tenant Lease

A credit tenant lease is a long-term lease on a triple-net (NNN) basis to an investment grade company—a company with a credit rating from Standard and Poor's of BBB or better. A commercial building leased on a long-term, NNN basis to CVS Pharmacy is an example of a credit tenant lease.

Commercial Bank

The word "commercial" is just a fancy word for "business." A bank that makes loans to businesses secured by accounts receivable, inventory, equipment, commercial real estate, and/or even just the good name of the business is considered to be a commercial bank. Bottom line: Just about every bank that you know is commercial bank.

Core Asset

A core asset is an essential asset for a business, an asset without which a business cannot carry on its main activity. For commercial real estate investors, their core assets are those commercial-investment properties that can be relied upon to stay rented and generate cash flow, even in the severest of recessions. Typically, core assets are Class A office buildings, R&D buildings, and retail centers that are leased to very strong tenants.

Crowd-Funding

Crowd-funding is the practice of funding a project or venture by raising many small amounts of money from a large number of people, typically via the internet. The difference between peer-to-peer (P2P) lending and crowd-funding is that P2P lending typically involves small loan amounts ($5,000 to $50,000), and just one investor lends the entire loan amount. Crowd-funding can sometimes involve much larger amounts, where lots of different investors chip in a little bit to make the loan or the equity investment.

Debt Service Coverage Ratio

The Debt Service Coverage Ratio is defined as the Net Operating Income of the proposed project divided by the annual principal and interest payments on the proposed takeout loan.

Debt Yield Ratio

The Debt Yield Ratio is defined as the Net Operating Income (NOI) divided by the first mortgage debt (loan) amount, times 100%.

Defeasance

Defeasance is the substitution of government securities for the property as collateral. A Borrower desiring to obtain a release of its property from the trust may purchase and pledge to the trust a collection of government securities that are specifically selected to generate sufficient cash to make all monthly payments due on the loan, through and including any balloon payment due on the maturity date. Defeasance is not prepayment. Technically, the note remains outstanding; but it is repaid from cash flow from the government securities purchased, rather than through cash flow generated by a property. The property is released to the Borrower free from the mortgage lien. In an interest-rate environment higher than the loan coupon, a Borrower may even be able to defease for legal, accounting, and rating agency fees. Defeasance is prohibited for at least the first two years following securitization, due to real estate mortgage investment conduit (REMIC) prohibitions on substitution of collateral.

DIP Financing

DIP Financing stands for Debtor-in-Possession Financing. The Borrower is in a Chapter 11 bankruptcy, and the Bankruptcy Court authorizes some additional secured financing, often to protect the assets of the debtor. Usually the existing secured creditors must subordinate to this new secured financing.

Doors

Apartment units are sometimes called doors.

Equity

In the context of commercial real estate development, equity is the sum of the capital that the developer has in the proposed construction project—including their down payment on the land and their prepaid costs, like architectural fees and engineering fees—plus any value that the developer has added through their efforts, such as assembling contiguous parcels and getting the property rezoned.

Exit Fee

An exit fee is a fee owed to a commercial real estate Lender when a loan pays off, regardless of whether the loan is paid off early, late, or exactly at maturity. It's like a prepayment penalty that cannot be avoided. It is a way for a commercial Lender to earn a higher yield without raising the interest rate so high that the monthly payments destroy the Borrower or without raising the points so high that the Borrower can't get enough proceeds from the loan.

Experience-Based Retail

Experience-based retail is shopping that is fun, interesting, and intellectually-stimulating, where the retailer often provides extraordinary service and where the center often provides dining and/or entertainment.

FinTech

FinTech is short for financial technology. FinTech is a line of business based on using software to provide financial services. Financial technology companies are generally startups founded with the purpose of disrupting incumbent financial systems and corporations that rely less on software. Peer-to-peer Lenders and crowd-funding companies are examples of FinTech companies.

Fix and Flip Loans

A fix and flip loan is a short-term loan used to acquire a one to four-family dwelling and then to renovate it in anticipation of an immediate sale.

Floaters

Floaters are adjustable rate commercial mortgage loans with a term of usually only five years. Floaters are typically large commercial loans written on conduit-quality commercial properties. They are usually readjusted monthly according to changes in one-month London Interbank Offer Rate (LIBOR). A typical margin is 300–400 basis points. During the fear and confusion of the Great Recession, when conduit lending almost completely dried up, floaters were made by the large money center banks instead to tide the Borrowers over until calm returned to the market.

Forward Takeout Commitment

A forward takeout commitment is a letter from life insurance company or other bankable commercial mortgage Lender promising to provide a takeout loan, upon request of the Borrower, 12–24 months in the future. All forward takeout commitments contain conditions, the most important of which is that the property be built in a workmanlike manner according to the plans and specifications and that the property be at least 90–95% leased out at the projected rents or higher. Forward takeout commitments typically cost the Borrower, just for the letter, 1–2 points at the time of issuance, plus an additional 0.5–1.0 point if the Borrower eventually asks the Lender to fund his loan. Forward takeout commitments are extremely rare these days.

Gateway City

A gateway city, as it relates to commercial real estate finance, is a very large city, containing over 1,000,000 residents.

Gross Rent Multiplier

The gross rent multiplier is defined as the market value divided by the gross (annual) rents of an apartment building. Put another way, you can roughly value an apartment building by multiplying the gross (annual) rents by the correct gross rent multiplier.

Hard Costs

The hard costs are a part of a construction loan budget. Included in hard costs are all the costs for the visible improvements, including such line items as grading, excavation, concrete, framing, electrical, carpentry, roofing, and landscaping. Another way to describe hard costs are the "brick and mortar" expenses.

Horizontal Improvements

To make horizontal improvements means to clear the land, to grade it, to bring utilities (water, sewer, gas, electricity) to the site, and to construct roads, curbs, and gutters.

Investment Bank

An investment bank takes companies public (issues initial public offerings) and maintains a market in the shares of the company.

Investment Grade

An investment is considered investment grade if it is rated BBB or better by Standard and Poor's.

Keys

Hotel rooms, especially in hotels with suites, are often called keys. This is a 200-key hotel. "Rooms" is a confusing word when a hotel has suite units that have more than one room each.

Loan-to-Cost Ratio

The most important ratio in commercial construction loan underwriting is, by far, the loan-to-cost ratio, or LTC ratio. The LTC ratio is the construction loan amount divided by the total cost of the project, the result being multiplied by 100%.

> Loan-to-cost ratio = (construction loan amount / total project cost) x 100%

Loan-to-cost ratios look like this:

> 86.1% LTC or 80.0% LTC or 76.4% LTC.

Obviously, the lower the loan-to-cost ratio, the safer the loan is for the bank.

Loan-to-Value Ratio

The loan-to-value ratio, or LTV ratio, as it pertains to underwriting a commercial construction loan, is defined as the fully disbursed construction loan amount divided by the value of the property when completed, as determined by an independent appraiser selected by the bank, all times 100%.

> Loan-to-value ratio = (fully disbursed construction loan amount / value of the property when completed) x 100%

Generally, banks want this LTV ratio to be 75% or less on typical commercial-investment properties (rental properties like multi-family, office, retail, and industrial) and 70% or less on business properties, such as hotels, assisted living facilities, and self-storage facilities.

Lockout Clause

A lock-out clause is an absolute prohibition against an early pre-payment.

Mezzanine Loan

A mezzanine loan is like a second mortgage, except a mezzanine loan is secured by the stock of the corporation that owns the property, as opposed to the real estate. Because stock is personal property and not real property, a Lender can foreclose on a mezzanine loan in just five weeks, as opposed to 18 months.

Mini-Perm

Mini-perms are short-term commercial first mortgages, typically made by commercial banks at interest rates that are much lower than those offered by bridge Lenders. Most mini-perms are written at a floating rate, typically at 1.5% to 2% over prime. Mini-perms typically have a term of two or three years, although occasionally a mini-perm will have a term as long as five years. Many times, mini-perms are written as interest-only loans.

Mini perms are most often created as part of a construction loan request. Rather than demanding that the developer find a forward takeout commitment (very difficult!), a commercial bank might offer its own forward takeout commitment in the form of a mini-perm. The advantage to the bank is that the bank gets to charge one extra point for the forward takeout commitment. In real life, the developer will seldom exercise his commitment for the mini-perm because the mini-perm has a floating rate. Once a commercial property is completed and leased, it's easy to find attractive, fixed-rate financing.

Money Center Bank

A money center bank is defined as a very large commercial bank, usually headquartered in a gateway city, which earns a substantial portion of its revenue from transactions with governments, big businesses, and other banks. A large share of the deposits in money center banks come from foreign investors and foreign companies. It is this access to foreign capital that gives money center banks an essentially unlimited access to capital. Most money center banks have either their headquarters or a major footprint in such economic hubs as New York City, Los Angeles, San Francisco, London, Zurich, or Hong Kong.

Mortgage-Backed Security

A mortgage-backed security is a bond secured by a portfolio of mortgages. These could be residential mortgages or commercial mortgages, but usually not both.

Open-Ended Construction Loan

A commercial construction loan made without the requirement of a forward takeout commitment is known as an open-ended construction loan. Most commercial construction loans made today are open-ended. Also known as an *uncovered construction loan*.

Pads

Spaces in a mobile home park are most properly called pads.

Peer-to-Peer Lending

Peer-to-peer lending is the practice of lending money to individuals or businesses through online services that match Lenders directly with Borrowers. It is sometimes abbreviated P2P lending. The important thing to understand about peer-to-peer lending is that no bank is involved. A single private investor is lending money directly to a private Borrower. The difference between peer-to-peer lending and crowd-funding is that P2P lending typically involves small loan amounts ($5,000 to $50,000), and just one investor lends the entire loan amount. Crowd-funding can sometimes involve much larger amounts, where lots of different investors chip in a little bit to make the loan or the equity investment.

Permanent Loan

A permanent loan is a garden-variety first mortgage on a commercial property. It will have a term of at least five years and some amortization; i.e., the payment will contain some portion of principal pay down. Most commercial loans are amortized over twenty-five years.

Portfolio Loan

A portfolio loan is a (commercial) real estate loan that the Lender has no intention of ever selling off.

Primary Location

A primary location, in terms of commercial real estate finance, is one of the most desirable locations in a gateway city in terms of traffic count, accessibility, safety, and affluence of the neighborhood.

Real Estate Investment Trust (REIT)

A REIT is sort of like a mutual fund that buys and operates commercial buildings. REITs are exempt from Federal income taxes if they pass 90% of their earnings through to their shareholders. Several hundred property investment REITs exist. There are also about two-dozen mortgage REITs that either make expensive bridge loans or buy risky mortgage-backed securities.

Rent Roll

A rent roll is a list of the tenants by unit number and the amount of each tenant's monthly rent. If the property is an apartment building, the rent roll will also contain the number of bedrooms and bathrooms in each unit and sometimes the square footage of the unit. If the property is a mobile home park, the rent roll will list whether the home on the pad is a single-wide, double-wide, or triple-wide. If the property is a self-storage facility, the rent roll will always contain the square footage of the unit.

Repricing a Commercial Loan

Repricing occurs when a life insurance company, conduit, or commercial bank—after it has issued a term sheet and completed its third-party reports—raises its interest rate on a commercial loan already in process. This normally occurs only after a significant negative event in the market.

Risk Retention

After December of 2016, sponsors of mortgage-backed securities are required by the Dodd-Frank Act to retain 5% of the offering in their own portfolios as an incentive not to put risky loans into the mortgage pool.

Schedule of Leases

A schedule of leases is a summary of the tenants in a commercial building that contains the (a) unit number or letter, (b) the name of the tenant, (c) the square footage of the unit, (d) the amount of the monthly rent, (e) the lease expiration date (and sometimes the starting date of the tenancy), and (f) any rent contribution paid by the tenant.

Scratch-and-Dent Loan

A scratch-and-dent loan is one that is flawed and has been kicked out of the pool of loans that some sponsor has assembled. Perhaps the debt ratio was too high.

Secondary Location

A secondary location is defined as a less commercially active area than a large city or an affluent, vibrant, and desirable area in a smaller city. A secondary location is typically a nicer-than-average location, but it is just not an incredible location.

Securitization

Securitization is the process of turning a pool of mortgages into bonds that can easily be traded in the organized securities market.

See-Through Building

A see-through building is a newly constructed commercial building, with no tenants and hence no tenant improvements. It is just an empty shell; and if you looked through the windows, you could see all the way through to the other side.

Shadow Banking

A shadow banking system refers to the financial Intermediaries involved in facilitating the creation of credit across the global financial system but whose members are not subject to regulatory oversight.

Small Balance Commercial Loans

A small balance commercial loan is less than around $5 million, although Freddie Mac's Multifamily Platform considers any apartment loan of less than $7.5 million to be a small balance loan. Commercial real estate loans larger than $5 million to $7.5 million are considered by most banks to be large loans.

Soft Costs

The soft costs are the construction costs that you cannot visibly see. Soft costs include the architect's fees, the engineering reports and fees, the appraisal fee, the toxic report fee, any government fees—including the plan check fee, the cost of the building permit, and any assessments—and any sewer and water hook-up fees, plus the financial costs, such as construction period interest and loan fees.

Standby Takeout Commitment

A standby takeout commitment is defined as a letter promising to deliver a takeout loan upon the proper completion of a commercial building. The terms of a standby takeout commitment are typically horrible—a very high interest rate and a big slug of points—just for issuing the letter, and another big slug of points if the loan ever funds. In truth, a standby loan is never expected to fund. It is issued merely to satisfy some construction Lender that a Lender exists to eventually pay off his construction loan.

Sizing a Commercial Loan

Lenders size a commercial loan by using NOI/DSCR; Interest Rate; Amortization to find PV. This is compared against the bank's policy on max LTV and minimum debt yield.

Structured Financing

Structured financing is a type of sophisticated commercial real estate finance that includes mezzanine loans, preferred equity, venture equity and joint ventures, senior stretch financing, A/B

Notes, and syndicated loans. Structured loans are usually quite large; i.e., larger than $5 million.

Takeout Loan

A takeout loan is just a permanent loan that pays off a construction loan.

Tertiary Location

Any location not deemed a primary location or a secondary location is a tertiary location.

Total Cost of the Project, or Total Stack

The total cost of the project is the sum of the land cost, the hard costs, the soft costs, and a contingency reserve equal to around 5% of hard and soft costs. Usually a commercial bank will insist on a loan-to-cost ratio of 60-80.0%. In other words, the developer must have at least 20–40% of the total cost of the project invested in the deal.

Tranche

A tranche is a slice of the yield of a mortgage-backed security. There are always various (6–12) tranches in a securitized offering. The buyers (investors) of the lower tranches enjoy lower yields, but they enjoy priority of payment if problems develop within the pool of underlying loans.

About the Author

Adam Petriella has participated in the purchase, sale, and financing of over 2,000 individual privately owned commercial real estate transactions in New York, California, and other major markets.

Currently he owns and operates a 10-person boutique capital advisory firm arranging debt for HNW (High Net Worth) sponsors.

He has had exposure to alternative asset management strategies and credit policies while running an origination platform he initiated de novo, within Waterfall Asset Management and its subsidiary, Ready Capital. He led growth efforts and managed day-to-day operations for the most profitable regions for a national, publicly traded commercial real estate brokerage company. His experience also includes an advisory role at Ackman-Ziff.

Petriella has successfully and sometimes unsuccessfully, bought, rehabbed, sold and invested in as an LP, numerous real estate properties.

Petriella is a Licensed California Real Estate Broker and a Licensed New York State Real Estate Broker fulfilling the requirements of each state as these licenses are not reciprocal.

Prior to commercial real estate sales and financing, he worked for well-known hotel companies Four Seasons, Westin, and Hilton.

He graduated from the School of Hotel Administration at Cornell University, following studies in business and engineering at Manhattan College in Riverdale, New York.

You can reach the author at apetriella@silverthreadcapital.com or through SilverthreadCapital.com.

NOTES

_____

_____

_____

_____

_____

_____

_____

_____

_____

_____

_____

_____

_____

_____

_____

_____

_____

_____

_____

_____

_____

_____

_____

_____

NOTES

_____

_____

_____

_____

_____

_____

_____

_____

_____

_____

_____

_____

_____

_____

_____

_____

_____

_____

_____

_____

_____

_____

_____

NOTES

_____

_____

_____

_____

_____

_____

_____

_____

_____

_____

_____

_____

_____

_____

_____

_____

_____

_____

_____

_____

_____

_____

_____

_____

NOTES

NOTES

NOTES